I0065517

Advance Praise for *The Ch*

Kris Cone's book had me hooked and nodding my head in agreement from the first page. If you have not been championed in the past, this book will have you not just see the value in having champions in your own life, but it will also have you see both the opportunity and value in stepping into being a champion leader yourself. If you are someone who considers themselves a leader, then you will get an opportunity to expand what it looks like to truly be a champion in a world that, as Kris highlights, desperately needs more champion leaders.

—Sam Kukathas, Founder of Soul Purpose Leaders

The topic of being a Champion Leader was super interesting and applicable to anyone, even me, someone who is not actively in a leadership role. This book is well-researched and well-planned, a subject Kris Cone knows well and is obviously passionate about. She's convinced me to be a Champion Leader!

—Micaela Eberly, Author of *Breakable*

This book is a phenomenal asset to anyone interested in building strong leadership skills. Kris gives incredible insight into her world of leadership roles throughout her lifetime and career by sharing real-life events throughout the pages. After spending countless hours swimming, biking, and running with Kris, I can assure you that her leadership skills are one of a kind!

—Anne Sharkey, USAT Level 1 Certified Coach, 80/20 Endurance Certified Coach, USMS Certified Coach

THE CHAMPION
LEADER

HOW TO FIERCELY ADVOCATE FOR YOUR TEAM, CULTIVATE THEIR POTENTIAL, AND CHANGE THEIR WORLD

THE CHAMPION
LEADER

HOW TO FIERCELY ADVOCATE FOR YOUR TEAM, CULTIVATE THEIR POTENTIAL, AND CHANGE THEIR WORLD

KRISTY J. CONE

ethos
collective

THE CHAMPION LEADER © 2024 by Kristy J. Cone.
All rights reserved.

Printed in the United States of America

Published by Igniting Souls
PO Box 43, Powell, OH 43065
IgnitingSouls.com

This book contains material protected under international and federal copyright laws and treaties. Any unauthorized reprint or use of this material is prohibited. No part of this book may be reproduced or transmitted in any form or by any means, electronic or mechanical, including photocopying, recording, or by any information storage and retrieval system, without express written permission from the author.

LCCN: 2024904100
Paperback ISBN: 978-1-63680-262-6
Hardcover ISBN: 978-1-63680-263-3
e-book ISBN: 978-1-63680-264-0

Available in paperback, hardcover, e-book, and audiobook.

All Scripture quotations, unless otherwise indicated, are taken from the Holy Bible, New International Version®, NIV®. Copyright © 1973, 1978, 1984 by Biblica, Inc.™ Used by permission of Zondervan. All rights reserved worldwide.

Scripture quotations by Holy Bible, New Living Translation, Copyright © 1996, 2004, 2015 by Tyndale House Foundation. Used by permission of Tyndale House Publishers, Inc., Carol Stream, Illinois 60188. All rights reserved.

Any Internet addresses (websites, blogs, etc.) and telephone numbers printed in this book are offered as a resource. They are not intended in any way to be or imply an endorsement by Igniting Souls, nor does Igniting Souls vouch for the content of these sites and numbers for the life of this book.

Some names and identifying details may have been changed to protect the privacy of individuals.

Dedication

To all those who have championed me, thank you.

To all those who didn't, thank you. You taught me resilience
and gave me motivation anyway.

Table of Contents

Note to Reader

I share many of the stories and examples in this book through the eyes of two fictional characters, Sarah and Scott, to protect the identity of the situations, organizations, and individuals involved. I've tried to maintain confidentiality and respect for everyone who shared with me while using their stories to illustrate key points I wanted to highlight. If you think you recognize any situations or individuals, it's purely coincidental, as the themes and characteristics are universal and widely recognizable.

I have included source materials for this book at the end page called Resources. I didn't use footnotes so it wouldn't interfere with ease of reading. Refer to these pages if you want more information.

Introduction

"Aunt Kris, why are you even going to do that triathlon when you know you won't win it?"

Jane asked me this while she was riding her bicycle beside me during my daily run. At first, I was a little put off by her suggestion that all my training was for nothing. Clearly, she did not appreciate the many hours I'd worked out over the past several months.

Then I remembered this question was coming from her six-year-old worldview.

She was not judging the work I put in; she simply wanted to understand my thinking. Instead of getting defensive, I tried to find an age-appropriate explanation for why I believed competing in a triathlon was more than just being the first one to cross the finish line.

I was training for an Olympic distance triathlon in Milwaukee, Wisconsin, an event with 3,000 people of all ages from across the U.S. I had qualified for this event a couple of years earlier but faced postponements due to the pandemic. While it was exciting to compete with this group of athletes, I had zero expectations of placing in my age group of around 110 participants, much less of winning it. My only goal was not to finish last in the age group, which I did accomplish.

I tried to explain to her that "winning" means a lot more than getting a gold medal. For example, someone doing their first-ever triathlon might consider that a "win." Or doing a longer-distance event for the first time. Or setting a personal record, or "PR," as we call it. Or just making a comeback from an injury or time off for whatever life event or circumstance that got in the way, and now you're getting back out there and training again. These are all "wins" that have nothing to do with being the first one across the finish line.

But to Jane, this was not enough. She only thought of winning as placing first.

I thought her view of winning was too small.

A Too-Narrow Perspective

We do the same thing for the word "champion."

To us, that word brings to mind images of being the first one across the finish line. The one to achieve first place. The top choice. Best in show. Receiving the award. The valedictorian. First in class. Any kind of "win" that means being Number One.

But this common definition is too narrow.

It presumes a zero-sum game where there is only one winner, which means everyone else is a loser. It invokes a dualistic mindset of "win" or "lose" where there is no nuance to consider the many other ways one can win. Or we can go to the other extreme where "everyone's a winner" gets a participant ribbon.

Regardless, using these extreme definitions causes us to miss out on arguably the greater, more profound, and powerful expression of the word "champion."

The truth is, if I only competed in events when I thought I would cross the finish line first, I would never sign up. And probably 2,800 of those 3,000 competitors in Milwaukee wouldn't either—the remaining 200 arguably have a chance of actually crossing the line first. Over time, the lack of interest would cause these events to stop happening altogether.

In this book, I want to explore a broader definition of the word "champion" and invite you to rethink what it means to be a Champion Leader.

Spoiler alert: it's not the one to cross the finish line first.

Missing the Meaning in Leadership

A lot of people aspire to positions of leadership. But when they finally get there, they may find out it's not all they thought it would be.

The additional challenges and responsibilities of the new role can be disappointing when they realize how little time there actually is to deploy all the leadership tips and tricks they've collected over the years.

And if they pursued a leadership position for the wrong reasons, such as stroking their ego through the prestige of a promotion or thinking primarily of the short-term benefits without considering the longer-term ramifications, it can leave them wanting.

All this can result in a meaningless leadership experience for both the leader and those they lead.

The World Needs More Champion Leaders

The world is saturated with leaders stuck in meaningless, ego-driven echo chambers. We don't need any more. Instead, the world is desperate for more Champion Leaders—individuals inspired and driven to invest in something and someone greater than themselves.

Who identify and cultivate the talent and potential in others for the betterment of a larger cause.

Who become the fierce advocate for the ideas, potential, and skills their team and the world needs to solve its greatest problems and challenges.

I believe becoming a Champion Leader is the most critical and impactful thing you can do for yourself, your workplace, and your world.

This is why I wanted to write this book.

My Journey

I have benefitted from having key people who championed me during challenging situations and turning points in my life and career. They were engaged and influential, and their value and contribution were immeasurable. I have never forgotten their selfless investment in me.

But there were other times when I wished I had a champion to support me. My journey certainly would've been less bumpy, and I probably could have avoided some pitfalls and roadblocks if I had more consistent, committed advocates along the way.

That's what makes the message in this book so important.

Someone who has a champion or has been championed is more likely to endure the seasons of difficulty and respond with greater resilience and confidence just because they have someone in their corner who believes in them.

From my experience, it's more difficult to succeed in the world without a champion. Or, as I like to say, it's hard to beat the championed.

This is the critical need I'm trying to address in this book: the world needs more Champion Leaders who will champion tomorrow's leaders.

> "You are where you are today because you stand on somebody's shoulders. And wherever you are heading, you cannot get there yourself. If you stand on the shoulders of others, you have a reciprocal responsibility to live your life so that others may stand on your shoulders. It's the quid pro quo of life. We exist temporarily through what we take, but we live forever through what we give."
>
> —Vernon Jordan, lawyer and activist,
> 2002 speech at Howard University

If you picked up this book in search of the latest research on management theory, a new productivity tactic, or novel leadership strategies, you'll be disappointed. That has already been written about in countless leadership books out there.

What is The Champion Leader about? Here's the summary:

Number 1: Our commonly used definition of "champion" is too small.

Number 2: Thus, we often use it in this small way and miss out on using a bigger, more powerful meaning.

Number 3: We need to become Champion Leaders and fiercely advocate for our teams.

In the following pages, I will:

- explore what a Champion Leader looks like

- challenge you to become a fierce advocate for people, ideas, and talent

- give you the strategies to solve the inevitable challenges and create better outcomes in a sustainable way

My approach might seem decidedly old school, and perhaps my strategies feel like common sense. But since Champion Leaders are still too rare in the world, these points are worth further review and study.

Are you ready to become the Champion Leader that your team needs?

Let's get started.

CHAPTER ONE

What is a Champion?

You were born with the opportunity to change someone's life.
Don't ever waste that.

—Author Unknown

Let's start by looking at the definition of "champion." According to dictionary.com (accessed December 10, 2023), there are five points of the noun form of the word "champion:"

- A person who has defeated all opponents in a competition or a series of competitions so as to hold first place.

- Anything that takes first place in a competition.

- An animal that has won a certain number of points in officially recognized shows.

- A person who fights for or defends any person or cause.

- A fighter or warrior.

Notice how the first three points represent the common definition of being the "winner." You have to get to the fourth point to find the definition I want to focus on: "a person who fights for or defends any person or cause."

Similar words include: advocate, ally, backer, endorser, proponent, protector, and supporter.

The verb form of the word means "to act as a champion of; defend; support." Per Thesaurus.com (accessed December 10, 2023), some of the synonyms include: to espouse, fight for, promote, uphold.

Interestingly, thesaurus.com also lists several phrases it calls "weak matches:"

- Go to bat for.

- Plead for.

- Put in a good word for.

- Side with.

- Stand behind.

- Stand up for.

However, I think these statements are perfect matches for what a champion is.

Think about it: if you are facing a difficult situation, wouldn't you want someone to go to bat for you? Whether times are good or bad, wouldn't you prefer to have someone put in a good word for you? To stand up for you?

Isn't this just another way of saying "Servant Leadership"?

What About Servant Leadership?

There's been a lot researched and written about servant leadership, and it's a valuable and potentially transformative approach. A simple description of a servant leader is someone who prioritizes the well-being and development of their team members by providing support, guidance, and opportunities for professional development. This leadership approach is characterized by humility, empathy, and a focus on serving the needs of others before one's own.

That last sentence holds the key: putting others first. There is absolutely nothing wrong with putting others first. It's a popular philosophy that has been espoused by religious and cultural leaders throughout history.

A Champion Leader is something different.

A Champion Leader is someone who passionately and assertively supports a cause, idea, or the interests of a group. This leadership style is characterized by strong advocacy, bold action, and a commitment to pushing for the success and well-being of those they champion.

The Champion Leader is assertive. Passionate. Active.

The servant leader approach feels more passive. Almost martyr-like.

The Champion Leader doesn't lose themselves in the advocacy and support of others.

Here are some other ways the two leadership approaches differ:

Different Focus
Servant Leader: focuses on the well-being and development of their team members.

Champion Leader: focuses on advocating for a cause, idea, or the interests of a group.

Different Approach
Servant Leader: collaborative and supportive, emphasizing empowerment and mentorship.

Champion Leader: assertive and passionate, often taking a more directive and advocacy-driven approach.

Different Leadership Style
Servant Leader: humble, empathetic, and service-oriented.

Champion Leader: bold, assertive, and passionate about their cause.

Different Goal
Servant Leader: team and individual growth and success.

Champion Leader: success or advancement of a cause, idea, or group.

So, while both leadership styles aim to contribute to the success and well-being of others, they do it through different approaches:

- Servant leaders focus on the personal and professional growth of their team members.

- Champion Leaders are fierce advocates for a cause, idea, or group, often employing bold and assertive strategies to advance their goals.

In reality, effective leaders do not look at this as an either/or proposition but will blend the best of both approaches in forming their own unique style.

Working Definition

To pull all this together, I want to define a "champion" as a "fierce advocate."

The word "fierce" contains the element of being a fighter, a warrior. The word "advocate" is one of my favorite words for describing the sense of active support or defense.

A Champion Leader is someone who fiercely advocates on behalf of another person, a cause, or something beyond themselves. Someone who is tireless and courageous in their advocacy and not afraid to make tough decisions and take bold actions to advance the interests of their team or organization.

Sarah's Story: During my early adulthood, my parents went through an ugly, public divorce in our small town. Following all that upheaval, my father was in another relationship and began broaching the topic of remarriage with me. Considering everything I was still processing, the idea of having a stepparent wasn't something I had even been thinking about. However, he shared something with me that, in hindsight, proved to be very insightful. He said something to the effect of, "You can never have too many people looking out for you," and encouraged me to consider his prospective new partner as another person who would be an advocate for me. I wasn't ready to hear it that day, but over time, I've come to appreciate the truth of the underlying principle. There's no such thing as having too many people supporting you, advocating for you, or simply caring for your well-being. The more people looking out for you, the better, and it's a perspective I've carried with me in all aspects of life.

CHAPTER TWO

What a Champion Leader Is Not

To build out this definition some more, let's talk about a few characteristics that are the opposite of a Champion Leader, which include passivity, indifference, and lack of conviction. These concepts overlap somewhat, so let's unpack them.

A passive leader may avoid taking a stand, expressing strong opinions, or making decisions and may not actively participate in advancing or opposing any cause. Why would a leader be passive? It could be because of general indifference.

Indifference could look like a lack of engagement or commitment to a particular cause or goal. An indifferent leader may distance themselves or display a lack of interest in the issues or goals of their team.

A leader who lacks a strong belief in or commitment to any particular cause, idea, or goal may not stand behind their decisions or the objectives of their team. To be fair, not every cause or goal requires a leader's strong conviction. A good leader should take a stand on some things but not everything. Ideally, the most effective leaders will strike a balance between which "hills to die on" and when to let go.

Scott's Story: We had a new division leader join our team, and his disengaged leadership style was puzzling. He was exceptionally passive, unwilling to make decisions, and just seemed uninterested in the role. At one meeting, I brought up a serious matter, hoping for a reaction of at least curiosity or maybe even outrage. Instead, he subtly dismissed the whole issue, saying it was the first he had heard of it, and moved on to other topics, leaving the matter unaddressed, which ultimately festered longer and got worse. In meetings where we needed him to make a decision so we could move forward, he often hesitated and deferred the decision further with a vague response like, "We should give that some more thought." We'd all been thinking and actively discussing the matter for some time; he was the only one who claimed to need further consideration.

We questioned why he even wanted the position in the first place. He couldn't make decisions and didn't seem interested in helping move the organization forward. Surprisingly, he didn't seem power-hungry or egotistical either. His motives were a mystery, just like his leadership style. I was happy when he finally left, he was one of my least favorite leaders I've ever worked for.

Principles that Guide Champion Leaders

Champion Leaders are guided by these five general principles in the situations they face:

1. Do No Harm
2. Know What You Don't Know
3. Give No One a Free Ride
4. Limit Star Player Bias
5. Don't Enable

Let's explore each of these principles a little more.

Do No Harm

A Champion Leader avoids causing harm.

This principle is loosely based on the Hippocratic Oath, an ethical code traditionally taken by physicians that emphasizes avoiding harm and prioritizing the well-being of patients.

The relevant passage of the Hippocratic Oath emphasizes an obligation to practice medicine with ethical consider-ations and to avoid causing harm intentionally. It reflects the broader principle of "beneficence," which means "acting in the best interest of the patient."

A Champion Leader aims to avoid internally causing harm or making the situation worse through their involve-ment or "fierce advocacy." Consider the ethical implications of your championing efforts. Make sure your decisions or actions align with basic ethical principles, including any guidelines or code of conduct your organization has, and avoid anything that could cross the line. You don't want your advocacy to open up the door to a bigger problem of ethical breaches.

Also, remember your role: you are likely not a licensed therapist, financial advisor, or medical doctor or have other professional accreditations that allow you to speak authorita-tively on matters that you are not qualified to. Stay in your lane.

Sarah's Story: I had a friend who couldn't understand the abuse and trauma I experienced in my childhood. As an adult, I started working with a professional counselor to address the aftermath of these experiences, and my friend was unable to offer meaningful support. Their own experiences seemed to cloud their understanding, leading them to suggest simplistic solutions like, "Why don't you just sit down and talk to your parents about it?" As a parent myself, I understood the desire for open communication, but what they failed to grasp was the inherent lack of emotional maturity and support in the parent-child relationship. The very nature of the problems and experiences I had indicated an unhealthy foundation, and it was unrealistic to expect a resolution with individuals still entrenched in denial. Explaining this to my friend became a point of contention in our relationship. They couldn't fathom why I wouldn't simply confront my parents and try to resolve things. Thankfully, my therapist reinforced my perspective—engaging with unhealthy individuals who caused the problems in the first place wouldn't lead to resolution unless they were actively trying to heal. I found personal validation in this understanding, but my friend couldn't bridge the gap in comprehension. Instead of being the advocate I needed, they were critical of my approach, and it marked the slow unraveling of our friendship. It was disheartening because I wished for understanding and support during a challenging period, but the relationship ultimately ended. Despite my desire for a different outcome, we reached a point where our differing views on healing and support became insurmountable.

Know What You Don't Know

A Champion Leader knows what they don't know.

This principle acknowledges that no one person, regardless of their expertise or leadership position, can possibly know everything. This gap in expertise can encompass everything from technical, analytical, or communication skills to decision-making, strategic thinking, and talent management abilities.

This principle requires a leader to have a strong sense of self-awareness and be willing to exercise it liberally, without hesitation or fear that they will be perceived negatively.

A leader who doesn't "know what they don't know" is one of the most dangerous weapons to their teams and their organizational culture. Why?

Their lack of self-awareness undermines trust and credibility, which hampers engagement and collaboration and ultimately leads to poor decision-making. If this pattern continues—which inevitably happens if a leader doesn't change—the impact compounds, resulting in a toxic culture that generates poor bottom-line outcomes. I don't know any organization or team that wants to foster a toxic culture that delivers poor outcomes, do you?

Sarah's Story: During an on-site program review, I was coaching a newer team member who was overseeing a crucial segment for the first time. I frequently checked in with them, asking questions such as, "Does this make sense?" or "Do you get this?" Their consistent responses included smiles, head nods, and affirmative words like "Yup" and "Got it," which led me to believe they understood the expectations of their responsibilities. However,

---

as the review proceeded, it became apparent this was not the case. While wrapping up the review, I discovered material mistakes in their work, indicating a lack of technical understanding of the assignments. All along I had been falsely reassured by what seemed like positive responses. I never really understood why they were afraid to ask any questions or admit they didn't understand something. Regardless, this was a painful experience that resulted in a detrimental outcome for both of us. However, I learned a valuable lesson that stayed with me throughout my career: ask better questions to gauge the depth of understanding and don't rely on nods and affirmative words as proof of comprehension.

A Champion Leader knows what they don't know and what they don't do as well. To compensate, they know the best people suited to fill in those gaps and are ready and willing to tap those resources.

When Champion Leaders acknowledge what they don't know, it sets off a chain of positive reactions. It demonstrates humility and makes the leader more likely to seek input from others, which in turn may make team members feel more comfortable speaking up to share their expertise. This trust and collaboration ultimately enhance the quality of decision-making. This impact also compounds into a more positive, healthy culture that generates better outcomes.

It's like having an alarm system and being confident it works.

In one house I owned, the smoke alarm near the kitchen seemed especially sensitive (or in this season of my life, I was an especially distracted cook) because it would go off at the first hint of smoke. This was annoying, especially having to open doors and windows on a cold winter day. But I always went to sleep with the confidence that the entire house-hold—and probably all my neighbors—would be properly awakened if a fire broke out.

It's like that with a leader who knows what they don't know; yes, it might be annoying that they don't know the answer, but you're sure glad the meter works.

Team members generally appreciate it when their leaders are honest about their limitations and are more likely to trust their guidance in areas where they do have expertise. Sometimes, that chirp, buzz, or deafening alarm is a comforting reassurance that everything is working just fine.

While this sounds so simple, knowing what you don't know is a powerful yet too rare quality that can make or break a Champion Leader.

It's a balancing act between wanting to look good individually and wanting the broader group to look good. The Champion Leader rarely struggles with this conflict. Their default is always for the greater good of the team. In order to get the greater outcome for the broader group, they can readily admit when they don't know something and instead focus on getting the expertise or resources to fill that gap for the greater good.

If you haven't spent much time developing your self-awareness so you can "know what you don't know," stop right now and work on this. I included a short primer in Appendix A to get started. Everyone in your life will thank you for your efforts to become more self-aware. Trust me.

Give No One a Free Ride

A Champion Leader ensures no one gets a free ride.

A free ride is when someone gets the benefits of being championed—opened doors, introductions, favorable recommendations—without actually doing the work or delivering the results. When a person takes advantage of the work, ideas, or achievements of others without contributing to the effort themselves, this is a free ride.

Yes, championing or advocating involves lending a helping hand and opening doors of opportunity. But ultimately, the one being championed has to do the work and earn that advocacy. They must stand up in the moment, perform as expected, and deliver the results.

A leader who gives a free ride to someone undermines their credibility as a leader. When there is a lack of accountability for missing the mark on individual capabilities or accomplishments, the leader loses valuable opportunities to foster personal and professional growth in their team.

"No free rides" also doesn't mean you swing the pendulum to the other extreme, where the leader creates additional hurdles their protégé must jump through to be championed. It will erode team morale when there is a perception that the leader is applying different performance standards and expectations of results across the team.

Bottom line: it doesn't serve anyone—the leader, the organization, or the one being championed—to advocate for someone who doesn't have the ability to back it up.

Limit Star Player Bias

A Champion Leader avoids "Star Player Bias."

Star Player Bias occurs when attention and development opportunities are disproportionately focused on a few star performers at the expense of recognizing and developing the broader team.

Every organization has a range of talent to work with. When the most talented team members inevitably rise above the rest, the natural tendency is to double down and try to capitalize on their strengths and exceptional skills. And why not—this focus can result in high-quality outcomes and outstanding performance in the areas where these individuals excel. However, a leader and an entire organization can become overly reliant on their star players, which creates a host of challenges.

For one, your star performers may experience burnout if they are consistently expected to carry the bulk of the workload. This can lead to decreased performance over time and potential disengagement from work.

It also leaves a lot of untapped potential. Besides just being wasteful of the potential, it can also lead to frustration, disengagement, and, ultimately, attrition if people aren't being utilized to their highest extent. People may look elsewhere for opportunities in an organization that is willing to cultivate and develop their skills.

The organization is also vulnerable if star players leave and there isn't sufficient bench strength to step up into the role. If the requisite diversity of skills hasn't been developed in others, it can create a vacuum that can negatively impact the productivity and success of the team. Having tunnel vision when developing the next generation of leaders does not foster prudent succession planning for the organization.

Even though star players bring undeniable value to a team, it's crucial for an organization to provide growth and leadership development opportunities across a diverse range of team members. When leaders recognize and cultivate the potential of their entire team, it ensures a pipeline of capable staff and leaders and mitigates the risks of depending on a small group of star players.

> **Scott's Story:** Our organization had eight divisions that were updating their leadership succession plans. The problem was that all divisions identified the same three names as their next leaders. Do the math—unless those eight divisions were going to consolidate into three, there were going to be five divisions without a viable leader ready to step in. It was like leadership musical chairs. Thankfully, our CEO called out this short-sighted approach. They challenged every division to identify and develop leadership talent within their own division and to stop assuming they could poach successor leaders from other divisions.

Don't Enable

A Champion Leader does not enable the people they champion.

The word "enable" comes from the context of therapy and refers to behaviors that perpetuate unhealthy patterns in a person struggling with codependency.

For this discussion, I think of enabling in a broader context beyond the psychological definitions. It's when the actions of others in someone's close circle of influence—such as family members, friends, or coworkers—though well-intentioned, may prevent that person from taking responsibility for their actions. As a result, they continue in those behaviors or actions that caused the breakdown in the first place.

In a leadership context, enabling someone creates a host of negative consequences.

For one thing, it fosters a culture of poor accountability. If a team member does not take responsibility for their actions, it's likely a reflection of their weak character development. If they are intentionally shielded from the situation and aren't allowed to suffer the consequences, it completely erodes the fundamental principle of cause and effect.

While there may be wholesome intentions in trying to protect someone from a challenging situation or outright failure, an enabling approach denies that person valuable learning experiences. Difficulties and failure are often powerful teachers. But if you consistently protect someone from "reaping what they sow" (see Galatians 6:7), they miss the chance to develop problem-solving skills, learn resilience, and form coping mechanisms. The Champion Leader knows these lessons will serve them well over the long term.

Enabling someone can also create an unhealthy dependency on the leader for guidance on routine decisions or tasks. It's important for the leader to strike the right balance between when to step in and when to let them work it out for themselves. It might be easier and quicker in the short term when a leader provides the answers. But when individuals are constantly provided with solutions, they lose the ability to think critically and solve problems on their own. Independent critical thinking is like a muscle; it must be used, or it will atrophy and wither away. The Champion Leader understands that the team's critical thinking muscles need to be consistently used and nurtured so they are healthy and fit and ready to be deployed.

Sarah's Story: Our division was evaluating personnel decisions in response to resource constraints. One employee, James, was eligible to retire, and we were considering retaining him for a couple more years to help with the workload. He was productive but difficult to

---

deal with. In fact, his supervisor had escalated several instances of unprofessional behavior to HR over the years, and his personnel file had a lengthy record of incidents. James' supervisor had been bearing the brunt of his bad behavior and did not support retaining him. However, the division vice president overruled this objection and offered a retention incentive anyway. They defended their decision by saying that "James' productivity outweighed his bad behavior." Ironically, this incident happened during a season in which our organization was updating the code of conduct, and there was a renewed emphasis that we avoid enabling or rewarding bad behavior. James' supervisor felt undermined that their recommendation was overruled in what seemed like direct opposition to the code of conduct. If our organization was supposed to avoid enabling and rewarding bad behavior, then why did we make this decision? The fallout of this decision was immense, and the division vice president lost a lot of trust and credibility in the process.

It can be a fine line between what is or is not enabling. The Champion Leader is a fully supportive advocate, but they don't ignore inadequate results or poor behavior they know will create negative outcomes in the long term.

Ultimately, these five principles form the guardrails along the ideal path of fiercely advocating for someone. Certainly, there can be some gray areas, but these principles define the boundaries that the Champion Leader knows not to cross.

Which one will you work on first?

CHAPTER THREE

What to Champion

Now that we've defined what The Champion Leader is and is not, and the general principles they adhere to, let's consider what the Champion Leader is supposed to champion.

What should the Champion Leader be a fierce advocate for?

What is it that they should support, endorse, and cultivate?

The answer to these questions is deeply personal for each person based on their own worldview and specific individual context. There are many great things to champion, such as ideas, talent, skills, and track records.

Sarah's Story: I was responsible for overseeing one of our IT programs and ensuring we had consistent proficiency across the team. To do this, I had to keep a steady pipeline of newer employees who were willing to learn a baseline of necessary skills. James was a newer employee who expressed some interest but was concerned it would delay his primary career goals. Despite his initial reluctance, James eventually got involved. After he surpassed the minimum proficiency levels, his interest grew, and he developed an aptitude for the topic. Over the years, he became an expert in the office and eventually took over the program management role from me. Years later, while cleaning out old files, I stumbled upon the initial survey and shared it with him. We laughed about his initial hesitation and acknowledged how far he had come. He expressed gratitude for my advocacy and support, recognizing the pivotal role it played in helping him find his niche. Eventually, James left the organization and leveraged his expertise in building a tremendously successful career with another company. Playing a part in identifying and cultivating the talent that resulted in his growth and success was a rewarding aspect of my leadership journey.

Each of us needs to think deeply about what is a priority to champion. You may see other things beyond ideas, talent, skills, and track record in your world, so you must personalize this response specifically for you. Ideally, you will identify other qualities and initiatives that should be championed.

For me, it's "potential." Championing potential is so critical that it deserves its own discussion.

Championing Potential

I believe the true test of a Champion Leader is being able to see beyond someone's skills and talents and identify their potential.

Skills and talents are more obvious to the outside world. You can look back in time with the advantage of hindsight, see a solid track record of results, and validate that their specific skills and talents do indeed lead to positive results. You've heard the saying, "Hindsight is 20/20."

But this is the easy path. There's rarely anything new here, and it has limited impact.

Seeing deeply into a person and identifying their potential—what is not yet, but what could be—that's a whole other level of emotional intelligence.

"I See In You"

The Champion Leader looks beyond the visible outcomes of skills and talent and sees into their character and soul. They see something else, something potentially more, something that could be greater.

The Champion Leader acts on their insight with a championing conversation with words like this: "I see in you . . ."

Identifying potential requires a high degree of wisdom. There's an element of looking forward. It also comes with a great sense of commitment with a willingness to invest in another person, which must be backed up with discernment and sound judgment.

Scott's Story: One summer, I coached a middle school baseball team. One of the players had average skills but a great attitude. This player hadn't quite found their niche on the field, so we decided to experiment with different positions and eventually tried first base. They had a positive attitude and a willingness to learn, and over several practice sessions, they became more comfortable with their skills and gained confidence through repetition. It was fun to watch them transform from being an unknown "diamond in the rough" into a dependable contributor with excellent fielding skills. Their growing confidence in their skills, on top of their good attitude and work ethic, had a positive effect on the whole team.

Indeed, the bar is high for the Champion Leader, which, unfortunately, is why championing potential is far too rare in the world.

But the stakes are also high.

Though I've said this before, it bears repeating: the world needs more Champion Leaders.

And the ability to identify and cultivate the potential in another person represents the ideal of the Champion Leader. That's what I want to explore further in this book.

CHAPTER FOUR

It's Hard to Beat the Championed

A Tale of Two Paths

On a beautiful late spring afternoon twenty-five years ago, two young individuals graduated from the same college.

These two young individuals were very much alike. Both shared the same passion for learning, had been better than average students, were personable and—as young college graduates are—were filled with ambitious dreams for the future.

Recently, these individuals returned to their college for their 25th reunion.

They were still very much alike. Both were happily married. Both had three children. And both, it turned out, had gone to work for the same Midwestern company after graduation and were still there.

But there was a difference.

Having a Champion Is Power

Despite having similar backgrounds and aspirations, their paths in life diverged dramatically due to one crucial difference—having a champion to support and advocate for them.

The first person was diligent, determined, and highly motivated, with a natural curiosity and a thirst for knowledge. However, navigating the complexities of the industry on their own proved challenging, and they often felt overwhelmed by the uncertainties of the corporate world.

The second person was fortunate to have someone who believed in them from the start—a mentor who was an accomplished business executive and a champion in every sense of the word. The mentor recognized their potential early on in their career and took them under their wing. Their path was paved with support and encouragement from their mentor, who helped them secure internships and connect with influential individuals. With the guidance and championing of the mentor, they developed a strong network and a deep understanding of the marketplace. Over the years, their career blossomed. They became a successful executive, making astute investments and gaining recognition in the industry. The mentor's support continued even as they achieved success, always offering wisdom and encouragement.

Meanwhile, the first person struggled to find a similar champion. They faced numerous ups and downs during their career, and without a guiding hand to steer them in the right direction, they felt isolated and lacked the confidence to pursue their dreams fully. Though they continued diligent self-study and investment in their personal growth, without the mentorship and advocacy that the second person received, it was an uphill battle. They had the potential, but it remained untapped without the right support system, leaving them feeling unfulfilled and questioning their career choices.

What Made the Difference

Have you ever wondered, as I have, what makes this kind of difference in people's lives?

It isn't a native intelligence, talent, or dedication. It isn't that one person wants success, and the other doesn't. The difference lies in having a champion to support and guide you.

One of the individuals had a champion in their life, someone who supported and guided them through their career journey. The other, unfortunately, didn't have that kind of support.

• • •

This story is loosely based on Martin Conroy's well-known "Tale of Two Young Men" sales letter for *The Wall Street Journal*, which ran from 1975 to 2003 and reportedly generated more than $2 billion in subscriptions. The original letter claims the difference between the two individuals is in reading *The Wall Street Journal*.

I rewrote it to illustrate a universal truth I have seen consistently throughout my life: it's hard to beat the championed.

If you compare two people with similar skills, talents, and potential, the one who has been championed and invested in, the one who has been advocated for and supported—that person will have advantages and opportunities that exceed the non-championed one.

Something special occurs in the relationship between the champion and the championed. Whatever that secret sauce is, it aids the championed in rising above adversity, pursuing opportunities others may miss, and finding unique ways to succeed and thrive.

Having a champion in your corner is a distinct competitive advantage in the workplace and the world at large.

It bears repeating: the person who has been championed is hard to beat.

So, what does it take to be a Champion Leader? And if being championed provides a critical advantage in life, why isn't it more common?

These are the $1 million questions I will attempt to answer in the upcoming chapters.

CHAPTER FIVE

The Rules: Strategies for Becoming a Champion Leader

What does it mean to be a Champion Leader? What does the Champion Leader do?

I don't have a cute acronym or a clever jingle that's easy to remember. Just these four simple words: Be. Do. Mine. Model.

These four words represent the strategies of the Champion Leader. Let's explore each of them further.

Champion Strategy Number 1: Be.

Be the person you needed when you were younger.
—Ayesha Siddiqi

Be the champion you wish you had.

It's hard to champion others if you haven't been championed yourself. It can be difficult and potentially painful to give to others what you wish someone would have offered you.

But this is the only path for the Champion Leader.

Passing on the shortcomings of the poor leaders in your life is not a favor to anyone, so you must resist perpetuating these failures to the next generation of potential leaders.

It's our responsibility as Champion Leaders to defy those unhelpful, anti-championing actions experienced in the past. You redeem these shortcomings by doing the opposite when given the chance—by being the champion you wish you had.

Sarah's Story: My team once had a high-maintenance client who demanded a significant amount of time and attention from the Relationship Manager and me. At one point, we learned that the client had significantly misrepresented something they did. But the client somehow turned it around and blamed the Relationship Manager and, by extension, me. Then, the client went several layers over my head to complain directly to our Division Chief and accused us of a serious security breech. We explained that the client had misrepresented the situation entirely, and my boss readily agreed we didn't do anything wrong. But then management removed the two of us from the client team, saying, "We need to make a change." The Relationship Manager and I were confused as to why we were singled out from the team when none of us did anything wrong. It seemed unfairly punitive, and it was demoralizing to face the rest of the client team after this. And how did this look to the client? Who knows? The client probably thought we got what we deserved since they thought we screwed up in the first place. It just would have been nice to feel like management supported us, to have a vote of confidence instead of feeling like we were made the scapegoat for the whole mess.

There are many ways to apply the "Be" principle. You could:

- Encourage and support someone in pursuing a growth opportunity.

- Offer constructive feedback to help them overcome blind spots or hindrances.

- Identify areas of strength and potential using the strengths-finders approach (see the book *StrengthsFinder 2.0* by Tom Rath), then hone in on those areas to enhance their performance.

When someone knows you are genuinely for them, dedicated to their success, and willing to make them look good when the stakes are high, you are in a place to make a significant difference in their life—the sweet spot of the Champion Leader.

Scott's Story: My team member Brian and I had invested more than a year into a project when we encountered a significant roadblock. We both thought we had resolved this problem months ago. Yet, here it was resurfacing again. Brian started second-guessing himself, worried he missed something that caused this to get so far out of hand. Despite the frustrating turn of events, I wanted him to be confident of my trust and support in him. I reassured him we had indeed addressed this issue months ago and I, too, believed it was resolved. I made it clear I didn't blame him for the setback and expressed my continued confidence in his abilities. I sensed he took my words to heart and hoped it would contribute to a trusting and collaborative relationship moving forward.

A Word of Caution

The "Be" strategy may trigger a reactive, trauma-like response, where you think, "Geez, I wish someone had done this for me!" But don't let this reaction hold you back.

The reality of being a Champion Leader is you will inevitably encounter painful reminders of what you may have missed out on because you didn't have an advocate in your corner.

It can be easy to fall into a victim mindset with an attitude of, "Well, no one was looking out for me, so I'm not going to look out for anyone else, either." But it's just not a very good story. Imagine what Cinderella would be like without the Fairy Godmother. Luke Skywalker without Obi-Wan Kenobi. The Karate Kid without Mr. Miyagi. Wilbur without Charlotte. Harry Potter without Dumbledore.

A better story is one where you choose not to let personal grievances dictate your actions, and instead, you are the champion you wish you would have had.

A better story is one of resilience and redemption, where you punch injustice in the face, sound your "barbaric yawp" (think *Dead Poets Society*), and declare that whatever you missed out on will not have the final word.

The Champion Leader is committed to being the fierce advocate they wish they had.

Champion Strategy Number 2: Do.

Do not withhold good from those to whom it is due when it is in your power to act.
—Proverbs 3:37, New Living Translation

Do the good thing when it's in your power to do so.

Champion Strategy #2 is inspired by the biblical proverb that you should do good when it's within your ability to do so.

The Champion Leader understands the influence of their role and the authority it holds and generously deploys that power to make a positive impact. When presented with an opportunity to do a good thing, the Champion Leader doesn't hesitate. They do the good thing because they can.

> "Give people chances they'd otherwise never get. Leverage influence to launch others into their calling. Write recommendations that give people what they would never get on their own. Refer. Brag. Name-drop others on their behalf. I remember every person that opened a door for me. In turn, I've tried to open doors for others."
>
> —Mike Kim, business coach and marketing strategist

The "do" strategy means taking proactive actions on behalf of others, supporting, advocating, and promoting them. It involves seizing opportunities where you are intentional, observant, and decisive.

For example, extend a compliment whenever you observe something positive:

- "Thanks for your work on the x, y, z project. I can tell you really took time to understand the situation, and it really showed in your presentation."

- "I noticed how you handled the x, y, z situation and like how you responded."

- "It was an interesting point you made about x, y, z. That was a great observation, and it really added to our discussion today. Thanks for bringing it up."

These moments truly cost nothing other than paying attention and investing a little time to say a few words that warrant being said. Simply speak life into a situation.

It's not as important whether you do this privately or in front of an audience, but your sincerity is non-negotiable. If you come across as sounding forced, like you're trying too hard and making something up, it may undermine your credibility.

Scott's Story: As a leader, I had a small pool of money to give my team "spot bonuses" up to a few hundred dollars. The funds didn't roll over to the next fiscal year, you had to use it or lose it. So I approached it like this: one, don't leave any money on the table, which required me to be intentional about looking for reasons to give the bonuses starting at the beginning of the fiscal year, not waiting until year-end. And two, I defaulted to being generous in the amount of awards. Whenever I observed someone taking on extra work or going above and beyond, it was always the maximum amount. They were usually surprised, and it was always well-received. Sure, I could have given out smaller awards more often, and they surely would have appreciated those, too. But why not go big?

> It didn't take long before the team understood I consistently noticed and recognized their extra efforts. The impact of that on team culture was invaluable.

To use the "do" strategy, simply ask yourself these questions:

- Is there a good deed that can be done in this situation?

- Is it within my power and authority to act on that good deed?

Inevitably, there could be extenuating circumstances that require further discussion and perhaps a different response. Asking yourself, "Why not?" or considering the downside of acting might help avoid a less-than-ideal outcome.

But those situations are probably rare, and the Champion Leader has likely already considered the potential landmines anyway.

In most situations, you should do the good thing because you can.

Do For One What You Wish You Could Do For All

You've probably heard the starfish story before, but it's worth hearing again:

> A young girl was walking along a beach upon which thousands of starfish had been washed up during a terrible storm. When she came to each starfish, she would pick it up and throw it back into the ocean. People watched her with amusement.

She had been doing this for some time when a man approached her and said, "Little girl, why are you doing this? Look at this beach! You can't save all these starfish. You can't begin to make a difference!"

The girl seemed crushed, suddenly deflated. But after a few moments, she bent down, picked up another starfish, and hurled it as far as she could into the ocean. Then she looked up at the man and replied, "Well, I made a difference for that one!"

Adapted from *The Star Thrower* by Loren C. Eiseley

This story illustrates the impact of individual actions, which is the essence of the "do" strategy. Despite the enormity of the task, the girl made a difference for each starfish she threw back into the ocean.

The Champion Leader understands that while they may not be able to help everyone, they can make a positive impact by doing the "good thing" in front of them.

Champion Strategy Number 3: Mine

Whoever seeks good finds favor,
but evil comes to one who searches for it.
—Proverbs 11:27 (NIV)

Any fool can criticize, complain, and
condemn—and most fools do.
—Dale Carnegie

The Champion Leader mines for the gold.

The above proverb conveys the basic principle that you generally find what you're looking for. The Dale Carnegie quote underscores how easy and common it is to criticize and implies that's what fools do.

Layering these two together results in a leadership approach that proactively seeks the good in others.

Why Do I Call it "Mining"?

Mining, as in mining gold, is a metaphor for the intentional, purposeful action of excavating beyond the obvious to unearth something hidden. I intentionally use the term mining because it is distinctly different from just "finding" the good in important ways.

Mining is proactive and intentional. It involves actively seeking, exploring, and digging deeper to uncover qualities that might not be immediately apparent on the surface. Conversely, finding is more passive. It's when you observe and recognize qualities that are readily apparent without having to actively seek or dig deeper. Finding does not require intentional, deliberate efforts because the qualities are visible. It's simply pointing to the obvious.

In a leadership context, mining involves a more thorough investigation. It requires a deliberate effort to explore, ask questions, and actively engage with individuals to understand their unique strengths and positive attributes. The goal of mining is to uncover additional hidden strengths that might not be obvious at first glance.

Why do I Call it "Gold"?

Have you been in a conversation with someone, and their face lights up? When their presence, their energy, their entire being expands? When you see that type of reaction in someone, you know you're getting close to their "gold." The gold is what makes them smile, what brings them alive.

I call it gold because it's a valuable, sacred treasure, almost holy.

The gold in another person goes far beyond just the good qualities they have—it's the essence of who they are. The very innate part of their soul that comes alive when they are in the exact place doing what they are meant to do.

Someone's gold is rarely found. It must be discovered on purpose. Few are capable of finding it by accident—or worthy of holding it if they do.

Mining for the Gold

The Champion Leader takes a proactive approach to actively mine the gold in others. This looks like catching people doing something well, not just dwelling on faults, finding errors, or looking for areas to improve.

Maybe you won't discover the innermost sacred place of those you lead. But you can almost always find something valuable if you focus on mining for gold rather than looking for something to criticize.

When the Champion Leader mines for the gold in their team, it can generate a whole host of positive results. Approaching your team with positive intentions can help cultivate a more positive and productive work environment. Constructive feedback that is focused on improvement can foster a culture of continuous learning and development that motivates your team to do their best.

By actively mining the gold in others, the Champion Leader cultivates a positive organizational culture, which is a powerful tool for building strong relationships, boosting morale, and enhancing overall performance. This positive leadership style can also help avoid the negative impact and sideways energy of unproductive criticism, which hinders collaboration, innovation, and team morale.

Sarah's Story: When I used to teach at our corporate training center, I facilitated role-play exercises as part of the course. When the exercise ended, we had a brief feedback session, and invariably, the students began criticizing, sometimes berating themselves for the things they did wrong. I would stop them and ask them to first tell me three things they did well. Initially, it was difficult because they defaulted to the negative. But it was a habit I tried to form with them throughout the class. Sometimes, it was hard to find something good. Some students answered that "It's over!" was the best thing. And in some cases, that truly was one of the best things! But even that was something we could build from. I tried to encourage them with positive details, such as how they didn't quit when they struggled and how they tried to find a different approach—these were all great things to experience and learn in a safe training setting. Just showing them how they could find positivity in what they thought was a failure is an important lesson I hope they took away.

Champion Strategy Number 4: Model.

The Champion Leader models the way.

Modeling the way means being an example for your team that they *believe* they can follow and *want* to follow.

I refer to this as "attainable" and "aspirational."

Have you ever considered what your team thinks when they see you functioning in your leadership role? When your team observes you in action, do they ever say:

"I could never do your job."
"I don't want your job."

The first statement suggests they don't believe your leadership role is attainable for them—they cannot reach that level or would not be successful if they did. The last statement suggests they simply don't aspire to your role for any number of reasons.

Modeling the way encompasses both aspects—showing that what you do is both realistically attainable and something desirable and worth aspiring to. When a Champion Leader models a way that is both attainable and aspirational, it creates a positive and compelling influence for those they lead.

Let's unpack each of these elements further.

Attainable Leadership

Attainable simply means that what your team observes you doing as a leader is realistically achievable for them. When they witness how you lead, including your leadership style and the results you generate, it shouldn't seem so out of reach that they cannot envision themselves doing the same.

On the surface, having your leadership performance considered "unattainable" may feel like a compliment. But that response is more about your ego wanting its day in the spotlight.

If your team thinks they could never measure up to effectively do your job, it could be they don't feel confident in their skills or abilities. And there may be a legitimate gap in skills, which is why you became the leader in the first place. As their leader, you hopefully have insights into the barrier because you've already had to deal with it in various situations. Whether you're dealing with a confidence problem, a skills gap, or both, the Champion Leader is committed to developing and cultivating the potential of their team.

It's also possible that a team member believes they could be a better leader than you are. If this is the case, you need to determine if there are truly undeployed talents or if there is an attitude problem, perhaps a history of negativity. The former is a great opportunity for the Champion Leader to cultivate and possibly promote that talent. The latter is potentially a negative culture landmine that needs to be dealt with before it spreads to the rest of the team.

The Champion Leader aims to identify and remove any obstacles that make your leadership performance seem unattainable.

Make it Attainable

To make it attainable, the Champion Leader should demonstrate humility by acknowledging they don't know everything and by admitting mistakes. It's alright to admit you don't know something, and if your team has never experienced you admitting this, you should try it sometime.

This simple step can take off some of the pressure they might feel to be perfect. It fosters the sense that they don't have to know everything or have a flawless track record to reach similar achievements—it is indeed attainable.

The Champion Leader also makes it attainable by demonstrating their humanity. They let their team see them as professionals and as human beings who experience the same ebbs and flows of the human condition.

There is a fine line between balancing your humanity and remaining professional. There's an appropriate level of personal sharing that will differ in each situation. Yes, sometimes the leader will have to tow the corporate line. But when appropriate, your team should also know when you struggle or are disappointed. This will help them understand that a leadership role is not a magic pill that shields them from the unpleasantries of work or life in general.

However, the most important thing is for them to see how you react to the struggles, frustrations, or even failures. Ideally, you will have developed personal strategies to work through challenges constructively without becoming negative, disrespectful, or insubordinate.

The Champion Leader isn't blindly optimistic either, pretending there aren't problems. Sometimes, the best thing you can do is acknowledge the difficulties in a situation without falling into a sea of negativity.

Scott's Story: One year, we were going through an especially difficult season of resource challenges. We had more work to do than we had staff on board to handle it. A lot of initiatives were underway behind the scenes, but the staff wasn't really involved in those and, therefore, were not aware of all the efforts being made. There was an undercurrent of frustration that management didn't understand the problem and wasn't doing enough to address it. So when I had my annual division meeting, this, of course, was the 800-pound gorilla in the room. I decided to broach the topic head-on at the start of the meeting. Someone asked directly how we were going to

---

get our work done, and I admitted I didn't know and that it looked daunting. I shared some of the initiatives underway and acknowledged that some may work, some may not, and some might work long-term but wouldn't show results this year. But perhaps going forward, we could avoid getting into this situation again. Then I turned it back to them—how did they see the situation? The team leader later told me that simply acknowledging the problem and not coming across as ignorant or dismissive of the situation helped diffuse the collective angst in the room. It ended up being a positive, constructive conversation. I think we all came away more hopeful and engaged in meeting the challenge.

Aspirational Leadership

Being "aspirational" means what you do is desirable, something others would want to do.

This is when your team finds a certain appeal in your job or the way you do it. Something is intriguing or desirable about the role that compels them to pursue it for themselves.

If your team doesn't aspire to do your job, you must figure out why.

There could be many possible reasons, such as they don't:

- Want to deal with the politics of the role

- Want the public-facing parts of the job (public speaking, community involvement, dealing with unhappy customers, etc.)

- Want to manage people or deal with personnel responsibilities and conflicts
- Like to do specific technical aspects of the job
- Want the added responsibility, stress, or workload
- Want the commitment of time, travel, or autonomy the role may require
- Believe the prospect of a pay increase is worth the hassle

Some of these reasons are out of your control to change. You'll probably need to dig a little deeper to understand the context they are coming from.

Maybe they had a bad work experience with a task or leadership role before and never want to do it again. Maybe they haven't ever felt supported to step out and take a career risk. Maybe they are in a season of life with temporary obligations, so it's not a "never" but just a "not yet."

Be clear about the underlying problem. Is it a lack of confidence, skills, or execution? Is the reason influenced by temporary factors, or does it relate to deep-seated values and priorities that are unlikely to change?

Make it Aspirational

While they can't control all aspects of their role, the Champion Leader has the ability and responsibility to conduct themselves in an aspirational way. This means being intentional about how they personify and demonstrate various aspects of their role, including:

- **Optics**: what is visible to others when you are functioning in your role.

- **Verbal**: what you say while operating in your role or about the role.

- **Nonverbal**: your attitude and general disposition about your role and the organization at large.

- **Structural**: administrative elements of the role, such as pay, benefits, your direct supervisor, direct reports, and duties and responsibilities.

Think of it like this: you are a walking billboard for your role. When your team encounters you, if all they see is stress, if all they hear is negativity, if they feel worse off after crossing paths with you, then there is probably not much about your role they will aspire to. It's that simple. Although if this is the best you can get from your job, maybe you shouldn't be doing it either.

Making your role aspirational involves performing your tasks in an engaging and impactful manner and utilizing skills needed for the role that are appealing. This may include contributing to meaningful initiatives that genuinely make a difference or taking on interesting projects.

There are also numerous intangible qualities the Champion Leader may embody that could be aspirational, like taking the high road, showing good sportsmanship, demonstrating resilience after failure, or offering empathy and kindness to others facing difficult hardship or loss. When others see how you engage in your work, it can spark a desire in them to also want to be in a position to influence important matters, to work on intriguing projects, and make a positive impact on the people around them.

However, it's important to provide a balanced view, acknowledging both the positive and negative aspects. It's essential to be open and realistic about the challenges without overshadowing the meaningful work that others may aspire to. This involves managing the volume of complaints about the job.

Similarly, be cautious about how you express any lack of agency or influence in your role. People aren't generally drawn to positions where they have limited ability to make a difference. As their leader, you are in an ideal position to prove that despite challenges and difficulties, there is an important mission at hand. Whatever attitude or reaction you dwell on is likely what your team will focus on also.

Sarah's Story: Two members of my team were more than qualified to be promoted to a position at my level, which would make them my peers. But when a position opened up, neither of them applied for it. And both were stronger candidates than the person who was ultimately selected. My reaction was mixed. I loved working with them and was thrilled for them to remain on my team. Both had a legitimate season of life considerations where they weren't yet ready to devote more time and energy to work. But there was also more to it. Our division had some recent leadership changes, and I had a new boss. The transition had been a little rocky, and I know my team saw the additional stress and frustration in me. I'd always tried to be realistic with them about the good and bad of the role because I wanted them to think how they'd respond in my shoes. Their reasoning suggested they'd rather have me as the boss than my new boss, so they were content to stay in place for now. As flattering as this was, it caused me to do some soul-searching. Had I overreacted to the leadership change or overstated the challenges of the transition? Had I been too open about my frustrations with the direction and decisions of new leadership? I decided to try and be more balanced with our conversations, talk through ways to resolve the challenges, and let them hear me exploring constructive solutions.

Modeling the way encompasses showing that what you do is both realistically attainable and something worth aspiring to.

These four strategies bring to mind an important question: if being a Champion Leader is the ideal, aspirational thing to do, why isn't everyone doing it?

In the next chapter, we'll unpack what gets in the way.

CHAPTER SIX

The Rip Currents: Why We Don't Champion

When I lived in Northwest Indiana near the south shore of Lake Michigan, I experienced many types of lake effect weather. One of these new experiences was the phenomenon of rip currents.

Rip currents form when waves break near the shoreline and the water that is pushed up the beach begins to flow back into the lake. As this water flows back, it can create a channel of fast-moving water flowing away from the shore, the rip current.

Rip currents are more likely to form in areas where there is a lot of wave energy, where the shoreline is relatively flat, and in areas that channel the water flow. On the Great Lakes, waves come to shore every 3 to 5 seconds on average, which is closer together than ocean waves and makes it hard to recover if you are knocked down. Rip currents can form within gaps in sandbars, near shoreline structures, along piers and break walls, and near water outlets, especially in windy conditions as the waves get higher.

On a day with strong winds from the north or west, the National Weather Service would often issue alerts like this for the south shore of Lake Michigan that would pop up on my phone:

Beach Hazard Statement: High waves up to 6 feet and dangerous currents expected at Lake Michigan beaches. Impacts: swimming conditions will be life-threatening, especially for inexperienced swimmers. Remain out of the water to avoid dangerous swimming conditions and do not venture out onto piers, jetties, break walls, or other shoreline structures.

The south shore beaches are very popular visitor attractions, especially on the weekends, so warnings like this put a serious damper on the fun.

Why all the concern? Rip currents can quickly pull swimmers away from the shore into deeper water, and when caught in a rip current, often the person is not aware of what's happening. Their instinct is to try to swim back towards the shore, which is directly against a strong current. Also, the current is usually strongest near the surface of the water, which makes it difficult to keep one's head above the water. They wear themselves out trying to escape.

Rip currents are the leading cause of rescues by lifeguards at the beach. The United States Lifesaving Association estimates that more than 100 people die each year due to rip currents. The National Weather Service estimates an average of a dozen rip current-related fatalities and two dozen rip current-related rescues in the Great Lakes each year.

To stay safe around rip currents, there are two pieces of general advice. One is to just stay out of the water entirely. Two is to know the signs of rip currents and what to do if you're caught in one.

So, what do rip currents have to do with leadership?

The advice on staying safe with rip currents is also applicable to Champion Leaders. While you probably can't simply avoid getting in the water, you need to know what rip currents look like and what to do when you're caught in one.

Champion Leaders Face Rip Currents, Too

Similar to how a Great Lakes rip current can sweep an unsuspecting beach visitor into life-threatening peril, we all face rip currents that can carry us off course and keep us from functioning as a Champion Leader. There are three rip currents in particular that a leader commonly faces: ego, effort, and emotional baggage.

These rip currents can derail anyone in any endeavor and are especially dangerous for an emerging leader. Some will acknowledge the risks, do the work, and transform into more healthy humans. Sadly, some don't and never will. If you don't figure out how to identify and navigate these rip currents, becoming a Champion Leader will be very difficult, maybe even impossible.

Let's talk about each of these more.

Rip Current #1: Ego

Your ego can easily prevent you from fiercely advocating for others because it means you primarily look out for yourself. It is rooted in a scarcity mindset, which believes if I champion something positive for you, that leaves less positivity for me. It's a false, zero-sum game that will bring the entire cycle of advocacy and support to a halt.

The Champion Leader has an abundance mindset.

Average people have a scarcity mindset.

Let's talk more about scarcity and abundance mindsets to make the distinction very clear.

Scarcity Mindset

A scarcity mindset is a psychological perspective characterized by the belief that resources, opportunities, and success are limited, finite, and difficult to obtain. People who struggle with this mindset fear there won't be enough resources (such as money, time, and recognition) to meet their needs, which affects their approach to relationships, careers, and personal development.

Here are some ways a scarcity mindset may show up:

Zero-Sum Thinking: People with a scarcity mindset see the world as win-lose scenarios, where one person's success or gain means another person's failure or loss. This thinking can create a reluctance to advocate for or celebrate others' achievements.

Competitiveness: Since they perceive resources as limited, they may be very competitive, always trying to outdo others or prove their worth. Collaboration will be one of their biggest fears because of the concern that sharing knowledge or opportunities will diminish their own chances of success. This competitiveness can strain relationships and hinder teamwork.

Fixed Mindset: A scarcity mindset is closely linked to a fixed mindset, where individuals believe their abilities and intelligence are static. This thinking often makes individuals hesitant to take risks or step outside their comfort zones because they fear failure and the potential loss of already limited resources. As a result, they never grow, staying stuck in the same routines and techniques as they've always done.

Scott's Story: I once had a boss who ran our team like his own personal fiefdom. While I appreciated his sense of ownership and loyalty to us, he took it too far. When I volunteered for external assignments I found interesting and could broaden my skills, he took it as a personal offense. He seemed threatened that I had aspirations beyond his control. Over time, it became apparent he was interfering with my career development behind the scenes, always coming up with more reasons—they were excuses, really—that I didn't yet measure up. I finally got out of the stifling environment, but it involved the personal sacrifice of uprooting my family to a different city. Once I was settled in my new role, I realized just how oppressive this was, and his reputation for operating like a fiefdom was well known across the broader organization. I'm glad I got out while I could still make something of my career.

Abundance Mindset

An abundance mindset is just the opposite. It's a positive psychological outlook characterized by the belief that there are ample opportunities, resources, and success to go around for everyone. Individuals with an abundance mindset see the world as full of possibilities and are more likely to collaborate, share, and celebrate the success of others.

Here's what an abundance mindset looks like:

Optimism: Those with an abundance mindset approach challenges with optimism, believing that setbacks are temporary and that there are always new opportunities for growth and success.

Risk-Taking: Because of their optimistic worldview, they are more willing to take calculated risks. They see challenges as opportunities for learning and growth rather than as potential threats to their resources.

Collaboration: They are open to collaboration, recognizing that working together can lead to greater innovation, shared success, and mutually beneficial outcomes.

Celebrating Others' Success: Instead of feeling threatened by others' achievements, those with an abundance mindset celebrate and support the success of their peers. They understand that one person's success does not diminish their own potential for success.

Gratitude: People with an abundance mindset practice gratitude for what they have, focusing on the positive aspects of their lives. This gratitude mindset helps them maintain a positive outlook even in challenging situations.

More Abundance, Less Scarcity

The Champion Leader approaches their role with an abundance mindset, believing there's more than enough from which to fiercely advocate for everyone, everything, everywhere. Granted, there are legitimate limitations to one's capacity, but these just serve to focus and prioritize their efforts.

If your unchecked ego prevents you from bringing an abundance mindset into the world in general, or your leadership role in particular, then you should proceed with caution. It's going to be a difficult path trying to champion others with a scarcity mindset.

Overcoming a scarcity mindset requires consciously adopting and practicing mindset shifts. This involves intentionally recognizing and challenging limiting beliefs, acknowledging the potential for growth and collaboration, and embracing the positive outlook that there is enough for everyone to thrive. There are many resources available to assist with this: hire a therapist, take a course, read a book—whatever it takes to get your ego in a healthy place of abundance.

Rip Current #2: Effort

The second rip current that can hinder a Champion Leader is effort. There is no way around it: championing takes effort.

It takes time and energy, and moments of opportunity often come up at inconvenient times. You worry that if you pause to be the champion you want to be, you'll have to drop something else. How do you have time to be a Champion Leader when you're juggling dozens of other urgent fires all the time?

Scott's Story: One year, my annual review took an unexpected negative turn when my boss reached into a drawer and pulled out a handful of documents. He spread them out on the desk and began criticizing me, stating, "You're not a very good writer." I was taken aback because this was the first time I'd ever heard concerns about my writing, and I'd been on this team for several years. The documents had notes with feedback and requested revisions, except they had never been given back to me to handle. I know my boss is a busy person. But apparently, this had been an ongoing problem, and my boss never took the time to discuss it with me. So, I had been unknowingly making the same mistakes over and over, which caused my boss more frustration that all could have been avoided. Instead, I felt ambushed because I had never been given this feedback before nor given an opportunity to correct the problem. How was I expected to fix a problem I didn't even know existed? It really broke the trust with my boss because he came across like he was just too busy to engage with me.

Championing also requires taking risks. When you advocate for someone or something, you risk your own reputation and the general goodwill you've spent a long time building up. You risk getting the work done and meeting the expectations for productivity, quality, and efficiency. The effort and risks involved in fiercely advocating for others are significant headwinds that a Champion Leader constantly faces.

There are solutions to consider when navigating the effort rip current. One is to organize and execute around priorities, and another is to cultivate a forward-looking perspective.

Let's talk about each a little more.

Manage Priorities

This concept comes from the book *The 7 Habits of Highly Effective People.* In "Habit 3: Put First Things First," author Stephen R. Covey lays out a framework for managing yourself in a graphic called "The Time Management Matrix."

I can wholeheartedly say this framework is one of the most influential concepts that has benefited me throughout my life. Simply stated, it's about balancing the urgent tasks with the important ones. But executing this is anything but simple or easy.

Let's clarify what we're talking about.

Urgent: Covey defines "urgent" as those things that require immediate attention. We face urgent situations all the time. They appear right in front of our faces, and we have to react to them quickly.

Important: Conversely, "important" matters contribute to our mission and values. They involve the results we generate towards our high-priority goals. We don't stumble upon important matters; they require us to be proactive and take initiative, otherwise we are easily diverted by the urgent.

Here's the key: urgent matters aren't always important, and important matters aren't always urgent.

Being a Champion Leader, fiercely advocating for people and the ideas and potential they represent is important, but it often gets crowded out by the urgent.

This is the rip current of effort: it takes work, time, and energy to be a Champion Leader, and it doesn't happen unless you are intentional about making it an important priority.

Forward-Looking Perspective

Another way to navigate the effort rip current is to cultivate a forward-looking perspective.

A forward-looking perspective is focused on the future rather than dwelling on the past. This frame of mind involves envisioning possibilities for your team and the ideas they represent. You create a mental projection of what could be.

If you are preoccupied with the past, either dwelling on recent accomplishments, rehashing prior decisions, or obsessing over past mistakes, it will be difficult to champion the people or causes you are committed to. All that energy and backward focus will cause you to miss out on what's possible ahead.

When it comes to evaluating potential in others, however, there is a strong connection to how they've behaved in the past, and you must not ignore it. In his book *Necessary Endings*, Dr. Henry Cloud declares the past is the best predictor of the future.

> When you ask yourself if you should have hope for this person to get better, the first diagnostic is to see what has been happening up to this point. Unless something changes, that is exactly what you can expect in the future. The best predictor of the future, without other variables, is the past. (Cloud 2011, 94)

We're not trying to rewrite the laws of human nature to say a forward-looking perspective will overcome a questionable track record. But the Champion Leader is intentional about inserting themselves into the "unless something changes" part of the equation.

This means being someone who cares enough and is willing to take risks to provide constructive feedback about the factors that contributed to past results. It's not overlooking the consequences of the past or making changes on their behalf. By giving this feedback, the Champion Leader provides the necessary catalyst, the critical inflection point for someone else to make a change.

If this process were a series of dominoes stacked on end, the Champion Leader would be the one who tips over the first domino and allows the subsequent reactions to unfold however they will.

> **Sarah's Story:** Part of my leadership role involved assisting with interviews. When I contacted the candidates who were not selected to let them know the decision, very few ever asked for feedback. I remember the many times I interviewed for promotions throughout my career, and I always asked for feedback. Most of the time, my requests for feedback were never answered, but occasionally got a generic, unhelpful comment. In a vow to do better, I made it a personal policy to meet separately with any candidate who requests feedback so we can address their questions uninterrupted. Yes, this is an investment of my time and energy, but it's fulfilling that promise I made to myself. Few people took me up on the offer, but I'm always impressed by the ones who did. I remember one productive conversation in particular where they were so appreciative that I took the time to pour into them. It was very rewarding as a leader, and unfortunately, not every day is.

Be prepared, though, because not everyone will respond with an interest or willingness to change. Dr. Cloud devotes an entire chapter entitled "Hoping Versus Wishing," which details nine objective factors that help you determine whether you can have hope that others' performances tomorrow will be any different than the track record to date. I'll talk more in the next chapter about what makes someone "unchampionable," but this entire concept is key.

The Champion Leader takes a forward-looking approach by giving feedback in hopes that it becomes a catalyst for change, then leaves the response to the other person. It's this intentional action that separates the Champion Leader from everyone else, and it takes effort.

This is the rip current of effort that the Champion Leader faces.

Rip Current #3: Emotional Baggage

The third rip current that can derail a Champion Leader is the emotional baggage that has not been processed and healed.

Every person, regardless of how they grew up, how they were raised, or what life experiences they've had, has emotional issues from the past that need to be dealt with. This can include the gamut of big and small events and situations, from trauma, loss, grief, and abuse. Even successes bring their own set of emotional challenges, such as perfectionism or fear of making mistakes, unreasonably high expectations that are never satisfied, and a scarcity mindset.

Some people may have lacked the encouragement or nurturing from a parent that they desperately craved. Others may have grown up being told they were "good for nothing" or "you'll never amount to anything" and struggled in life wondering whether it was really true. Losses early in life may have forced some to grow up too soon and fill the supportive role for other family members despite lacking that critical support themselves. Negative self-talk, feeling not good enough, or having a scarcity mindset all pose challenges for the Champion Leader.

Whatever the situation, the lingering emotional aftermath can show up in detrimental and destructive ways at inconvenient and unfortunate moments. Feelings of inadequacy or unworthiness from experiences earlier in life can manifest in so many ways, such as insecurity, defensiveness and reactivity, drama, or being out of touch with reality.

Scott's Story: One time I promoted a team member and coordinated it with HR to give them an initial raise and later on be eligible for a second raise. What's interesting is that I was serving in a similarly structured role, but no one had advocated for me to get that second raise. It struck a raw nerve with me, realizing what I missed out on personally and financially, especially when I found out how simple the process was. In the end, I just decided it was better to give the positive benefits they deserved rather than repeat my experience. They didn't need to be punished for the mistake that happened to me.

Champion Leaders must address and process their past. Otherwise, despite well-intentioned efforts, they will face challenging rip currents that can derail their efforts.

The way to prepare for this rip current is to work with skilled professionals to process your past in a way that brings greater awareness, understanding, and healing. There is no shortcut for this.

CHAPTER SEVEN

The Reality: A Day in the Life of a Champion Leader

*In theory, theory and practice are the same.
In practice, they differ.*

—Yogi Berra

By now, I hope you've bought into the theory of being a Champion Leader. But a word of warning: putting this theory into practice can be hard.

It's like this Mike Tyson quote: "Everyone has a plan 'til they get punched in the mouth."

This "punch in the mouth" can take numerous forms as a leader. For example, I got to a point where I questioned whether someone could truly be "unchampionable." Yes, I actually made up that word to try and represent my dilemma.

What if someone doesn't want to be championed or is incapable of responding to championing efforts?

When it gets hard, you are forced to stop and reflect on what it means to be a Champion Leader—and if you even believe in the concept anymore. If there is so much upside potential for becoming a Champion Leader, why does it have to be so hard?

The Encounter: Leading the Unchampionable

You will inevitably face someone who seems unchampionable. The challenge then becomes trying to figure out why.

What leads to this resistance? What are the qualities, characteristics, or situations that might make someone reject the efforts to be championed?

Three things come to mind as potential causes: skills, mindset, and entitlement. Let's unpack each one further.

Skills

In the real estate appraisal industry, there's a concept of "highest and best use," which refers to the optimal and most advantageous use of a property that results in its highest value. The appraiser will evaluate the potential uses for a property and consider location and physical characteristics, legal constraints like zoning matters, or other economic factors in determining what would result in the highest value.

The same concept applies in a leadership context and involves ensuring that your team members are operating in their "highest and best use."

When you sense someone may be unchampionable, the first step is to determine if they are even in the right role given their unique skills and areas of expertise. Are they in a position where their strengths are aligned with their specific role? Does their role allow them to showcase their "highest and best use" and, in doing so, contribute most effectively to the overall success of the team and organization? Or are their best skills and personality hidden behind tasks involving skills they aren't as good at?

Sarah's Story: I once had a guy on my team who struggled with the technical parts of the job, specifically staying organized. He often missed deadlines and, in hurrying to catch up, often made incomplete decisions with his rushed analysis. I became frustrated with the situation, not just how time-consuming it was to routinely deal with this, but because this was a long-term problem none of my predecessors had dealt with. The thing was, he was a genuinely nice guy. When I confronted him about the errors, he was cordial and truly apologetic. I came away almost feeling bad about even bringing it up. I realized my predecessors may have faced this same situation—it's hard to hold the line on a nice guy, so no one ever forced the issue. When I studied the situation further, however, it became clear he was in the wrong role and had been for a long time. No one had ever looked at his kind, thoughtful personality and realized he was ill-suited for a technical and analytical position. He missed deadlines and seemed disorganized because he spent so much time talking to other people. He was relational, empathetic, and a good listener, and he should have been in a role that supported those skills. I think about a chaplain, career counselor, or even a greeter in a retail store—anywhere to showcase his kindness and thoughtful personality rather than being stunted in a role involving impersonal numbers and technical writing. He eventually left my team, and it still haunts me that we dealt with so many performance struggles simply because he was in the wrong job.

If someone seems unchampionable, make sure their "highest and best use" is strategically aligned with their assigned role. This one critical step might fix the entire problem. Getting this right can make or break individual job satisfaction, team dynamics, productivity, and overall organizational success.

Mindset

A person's mindset has a major impact on whether they are willing to grow in their craft. An unchampionable person may refuse to learn anything new, to take feedback, or to stretch their comfort zone. Instead, they will resist any form of change, staying strictly in their old ways no matter how inefficient or disruptive they may be.

"Unless you try to do something beyond what you have already mastered, you will never grow."

—Ralph Waldo Emerson

Some people have a small worldview with no dreams, limited goals, and modest aspirations. There's nothing inherently wrong with pursuing a "small" life. But if in seeking that small life, you are leaving a lot of untapped potential and unused talent on the table if your dreams and aspirations remain hidden in the name of staying small, the whole world misses out.

"We ask ourselves, 'Who am I to be brilliant, gorgeous, talented, fabulous?' Actually, who are you not to be? You are a child of God. Your playing small does not serve the world. There is nothing enlightening about shrinking so that other people won't feel insecure around you. We were born to manifest the glory of God that is within us."

—Marianne Williamson

If someone wants to stay in their small comfort zone and avoid taking risks, they might be unchampionable.

It's hard to champion someone who wants to stay small.

Having a growth mindset, as opposed to a fixed one, is a crucial quality in knowing who to champion. At the core, people have to want to be championed, so trying to invest in someone who doesn't have a growth mindset might be a waste of time.

For a deeper understanding of the "growth mindset" concept, I highly recommend the book *Mindset* by Carol Dweck.

Entitlement

An attitude of entitlement can cause someone to seem unchampionable.

Entitlement is the underlying belief or expectation that someone deserves certain privileges, benefits, or rewards regardless of whether these are earned through their individual efforts or contributions. It's the difference between something legitimately earned versus something demanded or expected.

Statements such as "You owe me," "I deserve it," or "I have a right to" feel like an undercurrent of entitlement. The phrase "Give them an inch, and they'll take a mile" is another expression of entitlement. There's a sense of greed that tries to force additional obligations.

There are many examples of entitlement in our culture. The "Karen" meme, initially representing a white, middle-aged woman with racist, bigoted views, has morphed beyond into all manner of perceived entitlement.

In the workplace, entitlement can look like:

- **Resistance to Constructive Feedback**: an employee views their work as already perfect and thus is not subject to constructive critique or feedback.

- **Unrealistic Expectations for Promotions**: an employee believes they deserve raises or promotions without demonstrating the requisite skills or performance standards.

- **Demanding Special Treatment or Privileges**: an employee expects certain perks or conditions without the basis of contributions or performance.

Staff who are entitled may have unrealistic expectations about what is allowable. Their sense of entitlement may lead them to resist corporate-wide standards or guidance.

Sarah's Story: One of our team members suffered a serious knee injury during a weekend recreational league tournament, which required surgery and a lot of physical therapy. Since their mobility was limited, the rest of the team stepped up to assist by adjusting assignments and workflows and even setting up alternate worksites and schedules. Everyone was cordial and accommodating—

for a while. But the recovery seemed to take much longer than anyone anticipated, and staff began to wonder whether their colleague was really struggling with their physical therapy or had become too accustomed to the favorable accommodations. How do you confront someone that they might be exploiting the generosity of their colleagues? Before long, other team members began to ask, "If they can get away with it, why can't I?"

There is generally not a clear line to cross into the realm of entitlement, which makes it difficult to identify. Also, an attitude of entitlement generally does not appear overnight but is more like a slow erosion of attitudes and expectations.

Similar to what the boiling frog story suggests, if you put a frog in cold water that is slowly heated, it will not perceive the gradual increase in temperature. However, a frog that is placed in boiling water will immediately sense danger and jump out.

Now, I've never actually tried this with frogs and don't ever plan to, but the concept makes sense to me intuitively. When you're dealing with someone who has a strong sense of entitlement, it often takes you stepping away from the situation and reflecting back in order to realize what you're dealing with. It may be helpful to seek an outside perspective to help you see how pervasive the culture of entitlement really is.

Trying to advocate for an employee who feels entitled can be difficult. If there is a sense that policies and expectations are not enforced in a fair and consistent manner, it can break down trust and undermine team dynamics, which in turn fosters resentment and strains relationships.

Encountering the Unchampionable

What do you do with the unchampionable? What if someone just doesn't want it?

You've already considered the "highest and best use" question, and if it's not an alignment problem, then what?

> **Scott's Story:** For many years, I had a close professional relationship with a colleague, James. Then James went through a series of difficult personal circumstances and began to pull away. It was hard to watch him struggle while navigating these challenges. I reached out to him a lot and offered to be a listening ear or to help with various tasks, but he declined it all. Little by little, our interactions dwindled to just whatever I initiated, which in turn dwindled because James didn't respond. When I reflect back on our relationship, it makes me very sad. I wish I could have helped support James through those difficult times, but he just didn't want it. He was unwilling to accept anything I tried to offer.

At some point, you've got to let them go. You can't want it more than they do.

This doesn't mean you permanently put them "out of sight, out of mind." But you have to adjust your expectations according to the situation.

There's a principle in Matthew 7:6 that is relevant here: "Do not give dogs what is sacred; do not throw your pearls to pigs."

Let's be clear: I'm not referring to people or their problems as dogs or pigs, as the text states. What it means is that you must discern who you champion or advocate for.

You will be wasting your time advocating for someone who doesn't want it, understand it, or appreciate it.

Save your time and energy championing for those who want it.

Ideally, the unchampionable will see you continue to live out the Champion Leader life, consistently showing up and advocating for the people, causes, and ideas that the world needs. You should always be available if they change their mind.

The book *Necessary Endings* by Dr. Henry Cloud has a helpful framework of three kinds of people he believes helps discern "which kind of people deserve your trust." This framework may help you better understand the underlying forces behind those who are "unchampionable."

CHAPTER EIGHT

The Edge: You Can't Champion with an Empty Tank

By mile 10 of the half marathon (13.1 miles), I was in a good place, but my running companion was not. We had been doing run-walk intervals for the entire race, and our walks were starting to get longer. My legs felt pretty good, but it was getting harder to start up again after the walk intervals. We had agreed ahead of time that either of us could separate as needed, and since I was still feeling pretty good, I took off. Three miles later, I crossed the finish line.

It was the first time in nine prior half marathons that I had run the last three miles straight through. In all my prior attempts, I hit a "wall" at 10 miles and fought mentally and physically to finish. Despite adjustments to training, race day fuel, pace, hydration, and gear, I had never been able to break through the 10-mile wall.

What made the difference this time? In this race, I wasn't running on an empty tank.

The Champion Leader's Edge

What is the edge that sets the Champion Leader apart from all the other leaders out there? What makes the difference between a Champion Leader that succeeds and one that struggles?

The difference is the state of your "tank."

I went into this event under-trained; my longest run was less than six miles. The one thing going for me is that I had started a run streak nearly three years earlier where I ran at least one mile every day. I was getting close to day 1,000, so I had a good foundation of consistent running, just hadn't put in the longer training runs.

The run was in Mesa, Arizona, in February, so coming from the cold, snowy Upper Midwest, I needed to adjust my body to a very different climate. A few weeks before the race, I began intentionally drinking more fluids and electrolytes. I increased my food intake, too. I arrived in Phoenix a few days before the run and enjoyed several quality meals.

In fact, I was a little worried I had overdone the whole fueling thing. By the time we got to the starting line, I was feeling a bit too fueled! Between miles five and six, I had to visit the port-a-pot because, despite the sun and the heat, I had to pee—something I had never done in my nine prior half marathons. Clearly, my tank was full!

Ultimately this intentional fueling and hydrating played out very well for me. When I crossed the finish line, I felt like I could keep going. This had never been the case in all my prior half marathons.

Upon reflection, I realized I'd run all the previous races with an empty tank.

In prior races, I had a good fueling and hydration plan for the day of the race and maybe a few days before. But those short-term tactics were not effective in getting me to the finish line. I needed a longer-term strategy of consistent fueling to get me ready for that event. I needed to come into race week with a full tank, not just try to patch together a miserable slog to the finish line on depleted reserves.

The bottom line is that I did not, and likely never will, run well with an empty tank.

This is also true for the Champion Leader. In order to deal with the challenges along the way, you can't just wing it. You need to fill your tank through consistent, steady, positive habits that give you what you need when you need it to execute in any given moment.

You Can't Champion with an Empty Tank

When I lived in Wichita, Kansas, I was friends with an entrepreneur who made his own barbecue sauce. Occasionally, I stopped by the shop to say hello and would soon find myself engaged in some stage of production, bottling, packaging, or delivering the latest batch of sauce. His father, who we affectionately called "The Dad," worked there, too. The Dad was a professional tradesman who had a quippy remark or thoughtful solution to all manner of life situations, formed over many years of honing his craft. One of The Dad's sayings that he emphatically declared while stirring a batch of sauce in the boiling cauldron was, "You can't sell from an empty wagon." The Dad knew that the only way to refill the "wagon," which was the lifeblood of the entire business, was to make more sauce. And nearly every time I visited the shop, that's exactly what he was doing.

I've taken creative liberties with The Dad's comment to make an important point here: you can't champion from an empty tank. The Champion Leader's "edge" is operating with a full tank.

In the words of my friend and author, Kary Oberbrunner, the Champion Leader "shows up filled up," knowing full well they cannot bring their best without a full tank.

An empty tank provides little to draw from in a time of great demand or stress. When they reach for that little "extra" to pull them through when their reserves are depleted, they will struggle and maybe even fail.

The Champion Leader knows when their tank is depleting, and they know how to refill it. Replenishing your tank requires three key principles: managing yourself, setting boundaries, and ruthlessly curating.

Managing Yourself

Managing yourself means self-awareness, self-leadership, and self-care. Here's what the Champion Leader needs to keep their tank from being drained.

Self-Awareness

I talked about self-awareness earlier, but I will summarize it here again: self-awareness means having a clear understanding of your personality, emotions, strengths, weaknesses, and motivations and being in tune with your thoughts and feelings. See Appendix A for a deeper discussion of self-awareness.

The self-awareness needed to manage yourself well and keep your tank full includes these critical principles:

- Knowing what you're good at (strengths) and what you're not (blind spots)

- Understanding your personal rhythms of energy and focus

Let's talk more about each of these.

Know Your Strengths and Weaknesses

Earlier, I talked about the real estate concept of "highest and best use." This idea is foundational to self-awareness. Equally important is knowing what you aren't as good at and then adjusting your expectations accordingly.

There are numerous personality tests, frameworks, and other resources available to help you understand yourself. I have taken DISC profile, Myers-Briggs, and StrengthsFinders multiple times, plus various other assessments. Each brings different insights that contribute to my self-awareness, although the results can vary depending on the specific context I am testing from.

It's important to see the results applied in real-life situations. I've taken these assessments as part of larger groups and have experienced how the different personality dynamics play out. For example, once with the Myers-Briggs assessment, the facilitator assigned two groups to plan a dream vacation; one group was the "High I's" (introverts), and the other group was the "High E's" (extroverts). The "High" designation means they scored on the extreme ends of that rating band. Within 30 seconds, it became vocally obvious which vacation would be more fun. In fact, the "High-E's" had broken out into a dancing conga line before the "High-I's" had even gathered their chairs together.

A similar thing happened with the DISC profile. The facilitator assigned two groups—the "C's (stands for Conscientiousness; values high standards, careful analysis, and accuracy) and "I's" (stands for Influence; often enthusiastic, energetic, and upbeat) —to write out instructions for cooking spaghetti. The "I's" will whip out five simple steps and return to planning a really fun vacation. Meanwhile, the "C's" will run out of time and paper because they keep adding more details to include.

So why does this all matter? How is this information useful for the Champion Leader? There are a couple of schools of thought on how to apply this.

One approach that StrengthsFinders generally follows is to pay the most attention to your strengths. Another approach is to focus on improving your weaknesses and the blind spots that can derail you.

I tend to follow a blended approach. I prefer to operate out of my areas of strength and focus on doing the things I excel at—my "highest and best use." And I try to surround myself with other people who are better at things that I am not. But I cannot ignore my weaknesses. They can be like the rip currents I discussed earlier. I need to know how to spot the rip currents approaching and how to react when they do.

The key to self-awareness for the Champion Leader is to know what you are good at and to be intentional about surrounding yourself with a trusted team with complementary strengths and weaknesses.

Scott's Story: There was a guy in our office who was especially good at evaluating deals. He could find the hidden landmines and concerns that others missed, and he got to the essence of the deal quicker and more

---

accurately than anyone else. But his attention to detail was lacking, so it was always a struggle to properly document his assessments. Once, at the end of a particularly convoluted and difficult project, he offered to stay on longer to help me finish up. This involved the manual clean-up work of pulling all the final details together in one place. It was a disaster! I had to redo his work, which took more time than if I had done it all myself. We ended up in a big meeting about his shoddy performance with all the supervisors so we could reset expectations going forward. But it continued to be a struggle. One day, it hit me that I was looking at this all wrong. Why did I think he would ever be good at the detail work? That was not his strength and never would be. It was like hitting my head against a brick wall, and I needed to stop. I realized we would be better served letting him do what he was good at—deal evaluations. I was better at mopping up the details, and together, the two of us became a more efficient and effective team than nearly anyone else in the office. It totally changed our relationship, too, because I accepted that his sloppy approach to details was never going to change, and I quit getting frustrated about it. Instead, it released him to do what he was good at. The tension between the two of us just evaporated when we both worked from our strengths.

Understanding Your Personal Rhythms

Another part of self-awareness is knowing the rhythms and patterns of your energy and focus.

There's a critical difference between managing your energy and managing your time. A lot has already been written about the concept of managing your energy in books like *Getting Things Done* by David Allen and *At Your Best* by Casey Neiuwhof. Understanding my rhythms and patterns of energy has been one of the greatest insights into self-awareness and has resulted in higher-quality professional performance.

I know that my best energy is first thing in the morning, so I start my day with the work that requires focused, detailed thinking. Generally, by 9 a.m. on workdays, I have completed a tremendous amount of reading and editing work, which matches the optimal energy and focus I have at the time. This jump-start to the day gives me a productivity advantage in my workplace. Typically, by mid-morning, I start having meetings that may consume large parts of the rest of my work day. By mid-afternoon, I've likely been in numerous meetings dealing with a variety of topics and problems, and I am less able to hold my focus. I've found this time better for one-on-one appointments or other meetings where I may draw on topics and priorities from the day in more collaborative brainstorming formats. If something requires my attentive focus, I often will wait to handle it first the next morning when my brain is clear.

Knowing your strengths, weaknesses, and your personal rhythms of energy and focus are key elements of self-awareness that help Champion Leaders manage themselves.

Self-Leadership

Self-leadership is being able to influence, motivate, and guide yourself toward your personal and professional goals. Leading yourself is key; if you can't lead yourself well, it's unlikely you will lead *others* well. It requires knowing what your goals are and being able to motivate yourself toward those goals by engaging in routine actions.

This one is highly individualistic based on your goals. You need to adjust your habits and disciplines toward your objectives.

Self-Care

Self-care is knowing how to recharge yourself, which means understanding what energizes you and what depletes you.

Do you know the kinds of activities and types of people that drain you?

There's a practice called The Examen that I learned about more than two decades ago. It comes from the book *Sleeping with Bread: Holding What Gives You Life* by Dennis Linn, Sheila Fabricant Linn, and Matthew Linn.

The Examen is an exercise of self-reflection that makes us aware of moments of consolation and desolation—what makes you feel alive or drained— that can be instructive or give us direction. The authors provide several sets of questions to use in daily reflection. My favorite set of questions is:

> When did I feel most alive today?
> When did I most feel life draining out of me?

After many years of asking these questions, I have become more aware of what it feels like when I am energized: how I act, sound, and carry myself. I am also much more aware of what it feels like when something or someone drains me.

Understanding your consolations and desolations is a necessary first step in self-care. But self-care means you're able to give yourself the care you need in any given situation.

So once you know what energizes or drains you, you need to establish a set of activities, places, or people that are restorative and restful and that allow you to take care of yourself.

I find nature and being outside to be very restorative and refreshing. This can look like being active, like walking, running, hiking, or biking, or it could simply be sitting quietly in the sun with a refreshing beverage and a book.

It's important to note that my list will be different from yours. You need to know what restores you and be able to engage in a cadence that works for you. This is the essence of self-care.

Self-awareness, self-leadership, and self-care: these are the important foundations that the Champion Leader needs in order to manage themselves well and ensure their tank remains full.

Setting Boundaries

The second principle for replenishing your tank is about setting boundaries.

I first learned about this concept from Dr. Henry Cloud. For those paying attention, this is the third time I've referenced one of Dr. Henry Cloud's books (and spoiler alert: it won't be the last), which is not an accident. His book entitled *Boundaries* is one of the most influential books I've ever read, and everyone should read it.

The concept of boundaries refers to the personal and professional limits we set to define our physical, mental, and emotional space and what we will and won't do within that space. Boundaries give us a framework to make effective decisions, including the ability to say "no." They help us distinguish between the responsibilities and obligations that belong to me from those that belong to others. Thus, having boundaries helps us maintain a sense of ourselves—who we are versus everyone else—so we can protect our emotional well-being.

Whose Problem Is It?

I learned a helpful framework in a graduate school leadership course I took many years ago, which has helped me apply the concept of boundaries to everyday situations.

On a flipchart in the front of the room, there was a rectangle divided into three identical boxes. Each box had a label: "my," "your," and "no," which represented the three possible answers to the question: Whose problem is this?

The key to this framework is to determine which box a situation belongs in. Is this MY problem, YOUR problem, or NO problem? Once you determine that, you can respond accordingly. Getting this determination correct is the key to effective boundaries and keeping yourself in a healthy, balanced place.

Here's how it works: Someone shares a difficult situation with you. It's about them, and your job as a friend is probably to just listen, be a supportive source, and if they ask, maybe offer advice—but this is a big maybe. Ultimately, you plot this situation in the YOUR problem box in the framework.

When something is YOUR problem, it is not MY problem and does not require MY involvement or interference. Yes, maybe I am a listening, supportive friend. But if it's YOUR problem, it's for you to fix; I'm just here to support you. It's not MY problem to take on. Boundaries don't let you take on problems that aren't yours.

Another example. Let's say someone shares a situation with you, and they want to complain. There's drama, venting, and no solutions offered. Unless the situation is one where you are directly responsible, it is their problem in the YOUR problem box. Or maybe they just want to vent, and it's not even a problem; it belongs in the NO problem box. Either way, these are not MY problems. When you know it's not MY problem, you can respond by making sure you don't get sucked into someone else's drama and take on problems that are not MY problems to solve.

There may be times when something comes to your attention that is within your responsibility, and you need to deal with. It is clearly MY problem, which means I am responsible either for the people involved or the results to be generated in this situation. It is up to me to fix it.

This framework of MY/YOUR/NO problem is a simple way to apply the concept of boundaries. It's discerning what belongs to you versus what belongs to me and responding accordingly. One thing I especially like about this model is the option for NO problem. It is a step of refreshing wisdom to realize that not everything is a problem that needs to be solved.

Ruthlessly Curate

The third principle for replenishing your tank is to ruthlessly curate your life.

Curating is the process museums go through to select, organize, and display items with the goal of creating a collection that is meaningful and cohesive. Curating your life is similar in that you make decisions and pursue opportunities, relationships, and experiences that collectively align with and support your personal values and goals.

Being ruthless can have a negative connotation when it describes someone as cruel or lacking compassion, but there is also a positive meaning. People can be ruthless about making necessary sacrifices, streamlining their actions toward their goals, and eliminating anything that does not further their purpose or objectives. Being disciplined, focused, and determined to get what you want is a positive expression of ruthlessness that doesn't involve being mean or heartless.

Going back to the museum example, since they do not have infinite space, they may have to remove old displays to make room for new pieces. This critical subset of curating is identifying what no longer meets the criteria for remaining in the collection and removing it.

Ruthlessly curating your life acknowledges that to maintain a meaningful, cohesive existence, not everything gets to stay forever. It means being intentional about what gets to enter your life and what gets to remain, then letting go of what is not aligned with your values or does not contribute to your well-being.

There is probably something in your life that you should stop doing. Not everyone or every opportunity aligns with your goals and values. And our goals and values can change over time as we gain wisdom about ourselves and clarity about our purpose. You must be ruthless about curating your life and removing whatever is not working.

Curating Decisions

How do you decide if something should be removed from your life? One simple test is to consider whether it is serving you in a positive, beneficial way. In other words, is there an upside over the long term to consider? This doesn't mean everything challenging or unpleasant should automatically be eliminated, but self-awareness and self-care require that you understand the larger picture beyond the day-to-day struggle.

Earlier, I talked about The Examen, where you reflect on the consolations and desolations of your day. If you do this practice consistently, you should begin to identify themes of frustration, stress, or other strong emotional reactions. Also, consider whether something is within your control to change or eliminate. If there's a stressor that is 100 percent within your control to fix, this might be an easy curating decision.

Also, consider the things you consume, both in body and mind. When you decide to get serious about healthy eating, there are some foods you have to stop eating. The same principle applies to what we allow into our minds, including media, entertainment, and even who we listen to for advice.

Curating people and relationships can be particularly difficult. "People come into your life for a reason, a season, or a lifetime," according to the opening line of the poem "A Reason, A Season, A Lifetime" by Brian A. Chalker. Some relationships seem to self-curate for reasons that are inexplicable. While this may help explain the underlying pattern of relationships, it does not make the experience any easier or less painful.

Unhelpful, unhealthy influences should not get to live rent-free in your head. People can get entrenched in an echo chamber, listening to the same voices over and over. Ruthless curating might require that you discontinue a relationship.

Scott's Story: During one season of my life, I had a two-hour, one-way commute to the office involving a car, bus, train, and walking. Four hours per day just commuting. I hated it. There were long, crowded lines for the bus and train, and I witnessed so much rude, inconsiderate behavior by unhappy commuters. By the time I arrived at the office, I was often already frustrated with the day. I would often ask myself why I was doing this crazy commute. My "ah-ha" moment finally came when I admitted there was no "why." The commute stress was because of our decision of where to live, and there was no compelling reason for us to keep living there. This wasn't anyone's hometown; no one had a connection to the local school or community, and we had no family or friends in the area. In other words, I was suffering for no reason, which is a bad kind of suffering. But it was also 100 percent within my control to fix. So we put the house on the market and moved where I had a more reasonable commute.

Your decisions about curating could also be informed by doing an experiment. For example, have you ever given up something for Lent? Or have you ever done an elimination diet, whether with food or something else? It could be the sugar detox, where you give up all forms of sugar. Or you stop eating gluten to see how your body reacts. One year, I gave up watching the news for Lent. That was more than a decade ago, and it became a permanent thing. To this day, I rarely watch the news, and I still do not miss it. This is curating in action.

Throwing Pearls to Pigs

Years ago, I heard a speaker named Bob Gerard give a talk about something he called the "Assignment Way of Living." Essentially, he encouraged us to give ourselves "assignments" as a way to challenge ourselves, overcome fears or weaknesses, or test if something is still adding value to our lives. He gave numerous examples of assignments, such as meeting new people, asking for outrageous things, or starting new habits. The Assignment Way of Living could help you ruthlessly curate your life.

I'll give an example of an assignment I once did. I'm an avid reader, and each year over the holidays, I would give my favorite books to my immediate family. Inevitably, it became a scramble to figure out which book I wanted to give that year, get them ordered (which admittedly has become much simpler with one-click Amazon ordering), and wrapped and transported to the holiday gathering.

The last time I did this, I chose three books that I painstakingly wrapped and tied with a fancy thick rope and placed under the tree. The kids were young, the gift exchange was energetic, and the books I had thoughtfully selected were lost in all the commotion. It then occurred to me I was the only one who cared about this ritual. So, I gave myself the assignment to stop the holiday book gift and see who noticed. The answer: no one. It's been many years since, and to date, no one has asked me about it. And since no one has missed it, the assignment was indeed successful in helping me curate an activity that no one cared about besides me. Plus, it saved hundreds of dollars to spend on more books for myself.

What assignments can you give yourself to help with curating decisions?

The Matthew 7:6 passage that I referenced earlier ("Do not give to dogs what is sacred; do not throw your pearls to pigs)" is also relevant to our discussion here. Not everyone values what you value, and therefore, the expectations around those values will probably be different. We should stop wasting time, energy, and money on people who may not appreciate the value of what they are being given. If nobody cares about this except me, maybe I should stop doing it. This doesn't mean we should stop being generous, but at the very least, maybe our expectations about the response to our generosity should change.

Sarah's Story: One year, I gifted my siblings a financial plan review from my certified financial planner. I paid all the fees upfront; all they had to do was show up. Using a CFP was extremely valuable for me, and I wanted them to benefit from my advisor's good work. Plus, my siblings all had kids and other factors to be prepared for. It seemed like a win-win situation for everyone. Except I was the only one that really wanted it. One sibling missed the initial deadline to respond and never even started the process. The others went back and forth with the advisor for a while but never got all their information pulled together. It started to impact my relationship with my advisor, too. The advisor gave me updates and was disappointed the process was moving so slowly. Finally, after a couple of years, the advisor terminated the deal and refunded me the money. Later, we both reflected on all we'd learned from the experience, including adages like "Don't throw pearls to pigs," "You can lead a horse to water, but you can't make them drink," or "It has to be their idea."

Having the Champion Leader's Edge is being able to monitor the state of your tank, knowing when it's running low, and, most importantly, knowing how to replenish it. Managing yourself, setting boundaries, and ruthlessly curating are the keys to maintaining this Edge.

CHAPTER NINE

The End Game: Leave a Good Wake

In his book *Integrity*, Dr. Henry Cloud talks about a concept he calls "the wake." I'll summarize his illustration for you here, but do yourself a favor and read this book for yourself to fully understand this point.

> You can tell a lot about a boat just by watching its wake. Whether it's going in a straight line or wavering may tell you about the attention of the captain or the functionality of its mechanical parts. If the wake is smooth and flat or steep and choppy may tell you about the speed or drag of the boat.

> The same is true of people. When a person goes through an organization or any kind of working relationship, they leave behind a "wake" in two areas: tasks and relationships. This prompts these two questions: what did they accomplish, and how did they deal with people?

We can tell a lot about a person from the nature of the wake they leave behind. The task side of the wake reflects the real performance and results they produce. On the relationship side, our interactions with people affect their hearts, minds, and souls. We leave a wake of people behind us as we move through their lives and their organizations.

The end game of the Champion Leader is to leave behind a positive, high-quality wake. Thus, the key question the Champion Leader should ask themselves is: What does my wake look like?

Here are some additional questions that may help you examine the quality of your wake:

- How would your team describe their experience with you?

- Did you leave them better off because you "moved through their lives," or would they say you left them worse off?

- Do they consider it a positive thing or a privilege that they were associated with you? Or has it been a negative or painful experience?

Another key question: Would you do it again?

For the Champion Leader, the telling question is whether your team would want to be associated with you in the future. Knowing what they know now, would they want to work with you again?

Sarah's Story: Once, our division welcomed a new leader who went around to the various territories to introduce themselves. When meeting with our team, they shared their leadership perspectives, and one particular comment about their supportive leadership philosophy really stood out to me. They proclaimed, "I would walk into a propeller for you." I always remembered that comment because of the vivid imagery it invoked. Years later, we faced a challenging situation, and as the scenario unfolded, it became painfully evident that what they truly meant was, "I will throw you into the propeller at the first opportunity to save my own skin." It was so ironic! The disconnect between their assurances and how they actually operated under stress left a lasting impression on me. I swore that whenever I became a leader, I would try to avoid making such specific, vivid promises that I was not willing to back up.

Epilogue

Life is long, and helping others when they need it often comes back to you in ways you least expect it.

—Stephen Schwarzman

I have not always had champions in my corner when I needed them. But sometimes, the right advocates were there in key moments. Let me tell you about one:

In my first job out of college, a colleague became a champion for me. From the beginning, she believed in me and provided unwavering encouragement during my formative years. She was a terrific role model and the kind of colleague you always wanted to work hard for. After a few years, though, I was feeling restless and began exploring options, including the possibility of going to law school. I was worried about mentioning it to her because it meant leaving the job, and I didn't want to appear ungrateful for all her support. When I did bring it up, she surprised me by not only supporting my decision but also offering to write a letter of recommendation. I know what it looks like when you support someone leaving that you wanted to get rid of anyway. But in this situation, I felt nothing but sincere support.

It was a gesture of a true champion who was genuinely interested in my aspirations and well-being, even if it meant parting ways professionally. I was accepted to law school but ultimately ended up pursuing other options. A few years later, we ended up working together again, and she was my direct supervisor for a while. Her fierce advocacy for me left a lasting impact and helped me realize just how critical it can be to have a champion. It also gave me a passion to want to pay it forward. And over my career, there have been many opportunities to do so.

One time, a person I had been coaching was considering leaving the organization. They reached out to me for advice on choosing between two job options: another role in the industry or working for the family business. I remembered how powerful it was to have someone advocate for me, and I wanted to do the same, even if that meant this person would leave the industry.

Eventually, a recruiter from the industry position reached out to me for a reference. While I gave a wholehearted endorsement, I was clear that my primary concern was supporting my colleague in what would be most fulfilling long term. They ultimately chose the family business, and all these years later, it seems to have been a great choice. Could they have made this decision without me and my support? Absolutely. How much did my advocacy matter in the final decision? I don't know. And it doesn't matter anyway.

I am a Champion Leader regardless of the outcome.

• • •

This book has taken me a long time to write.

It's my first book, so there's a learning curve to overcome. Thankfully, I have a great team supporting me with the expertise and inspiration to get to the finish line.

This concept is deeply personal to me, and it's taken a while to flesh out. The idea of being a Champion Leader has percolated with me for a long time, but I didn't fully understand it and didn't even know what to call it. So, I've had to unpack it, create definitions, codify everything, then put it into practice. Practice sometimes resulted in successful outcomes, but sometimes did not, which required more learning and revisiting so I could practice again.

But finally, I've pulled all the pieces together:

- Why the world needs more Champion Leaders

- What a Champion Leader is and is not

- Strategies for becoming a Champion Leader

- Obstacles that get in the way of being a Champion Leader

- Putting yourself in the best position to be a Champion Leader long term

And along the way, I've discovered my Massive Transformative Purpose, which author and entrepreneur Peter H. Diamandis describes as the "unique bold and aspirational vision of the change in the world that you want to achieve:"

Championing the World-Changers of Tomorrow.

This book is my roadmap for how I plan to do that. Will you join me?

APPENDIX A

Primer on Self-Awareness

A quick primer on self-awareness:

Being self-aware means having a clear understanding of your personality, emotions, strengths, weaknesses, and motivations. It involves introspection, emotional intelligence, and a willingness to learn and grow. Self-aware people are more in tune with their thoughts and feelings, which enables them to manage their behavior effectively and make more informed decisions. Self-awareness is a crucial aspect of emotional intelligence and personal development.

A few characteristics that may represent someone with good self-awareness:

- **Understand Their Strengths and Weaknesses**: a realistic perception and discernment that helps them leverage their strengths and work on areas that need improvement, which in turn supports their personal and professional growth.

- **Open to Feedback**: open to constructive feedback that they then utilize as an opportunity for growth; they recognize that external perspectives can provide valuable insights.

- **Emotional Regulation**: adept at recognizing and regulating their emotions, which helps them navigate challenging situations calmly and make rational decisions even in emotionally charged environments.

- **Adaptability**: adaptable and open to change, able to adjust their behavior and strategies in response to different circumstances, which demonstrates resilience.

- **Effective Communication**: mindful of their communication style and how it may be perceived, which leads to clearer communication and reduces the likelihood of misunderstandings.

On the other hand, these are some qualities that may represent someone who lacks self-awareness:

- **Deny Their Flaws**: denying or downplaying personal flaws, which prevents individuals from addressing areas that need improvement.

- **Defensive**: responds defensively to feedback or criticism, which prevents an honest evaluation of their behaviors or actions and hinders personal growth.

- **Impulsive**: struggles to regulate their impulses, which can lead to rash decision-making or emotional outbursts that negatively impact relationships and outcomes.

- **Resistant to Change/Rigid**: resist change and new perspectives, which can contribute to inflexibility or stagnation, resulting in difficulty navigating change.

- **Poor Communication**: ineffective communication skills and habits that can lead to misunderstandings, conflict, and strained relationships.

How to become more self-aware:

Becoming more self-aware is a transformative journey that involves introspection, observation, and a commitment to personal growth. Here are some practical ways to enhance self-awareness:

- **Practice Mindfulness**: engage in mindfulness meditation or mindfulness-based activities.

- **Journaling**: regularly journal your thoughts and reflections.

- **Seek Feedback**: actively seek feedback from friends, family, and colleagues.

- **Personality Assessments**: take personality assessments to gain insights into your strengths and weaknesses such as Myers-Briggs Type Indicator (MBTI), DISC Profile, StrengthsFinder, or the Enneagram.

- **Emotional Intelligence**: work on developing emotional intelligence.

- **Reflect on Values**: reflect on your core values and whether your actions align with them.

- **360-Degree Assessments**: use 360-degree assessments to get feedback from various perspectives, such as The Leadership Circle Profile or similar tools.

- **Practice Active Listening**: improve your listening skills in conversations.

- **Therapy or Coaching**: engage in therapy or coaching to explore deeper aspects of yourself.

- **Read Biographies and Autobiographies**: gain insights from the life stories of others.

- **Attend Workshops and Seminars**: participate in personal development workshops or attend seminars by renowned psychologists or self-help experts.

- **Reflect on Life Experiences**: reflect on significant life experiences and the lessons learned.

- **Peer Learning Groups**: join or create a peer learning group where members share insights and support each other's growth.

Enhancing self-awareness is an ongoing process, and combining various activities and resources can provide a holistic approach to personal growth. Each individual is unique, so it's valuable to explore what resonates most with your own preferences and learning style.

Resources

Getting Things Done by David Allen

Boundaries by Dr. Henry Cloud

Integrity by Dr. Henry Cloud

Necessary Endings by Dr. Henry Cloud

The 7 Habits of Highly Effective People by Stephen R. Covey

Bold by Peter H. Diamandis and Steven Kotler

Sleeping with Bread: Holding What Gives You Life by Dennis Linn, Sheila Fabricant Linn, Matthew Linn

At Your Best by Casey Neiuwarner

Do the Work by Steven Pressfield

• • •

Other excellent books I've read for personal growth and developing self-awareness:

Daring Greatly by Brené Brown: Embracing vulnerability and imperfection.

Atomic Habits by James Clear: Building positive habits and breaking bad ones.

Mindset: The New Psychology of Success by Carol S. Dweck: Developing a growth mindset.

Man's Search for Meaning by Viktor E. Frankl: Finding purpose and meaning in life and work.

The Subtle Art of Not Giving a F*ck by Mark Manson: Practical advice on focusing on what truly matters for a fulfilling life.

Essentialism: The Disciplined Pursuit of Less by Greg McKeown: Simplifying life and work by focusing on what truly matters.

Deep Work by Cal Newport: Maximizing productivity and focus in a distracted world.

Drive: The Surprising Truth About What Motivates Us by Daniel H. Pink: Understanding motivation and how it plays a role in personal and professional life.

About the Author

Kristy J. Cone is a seasoned veteran of the business world, having spent more than thirty years navigating the corporate trenches to the C-Suite. Throughout her journey, she observed a common thread among many individuals, herself included, with untapped potential waiting to be unleashed. But unless there was someone to help identify and champion that potential, it got lost in the frenzy of corporate and personal life, and the world missed out on what could have been.

Kristy's approach is shaped by a lifelong love of learning and commitment to personal growth, forming a distinctive blend of wisdom and leadership that she leverages in helping others live out their highest potential. With expertise in strategic thinking, problem-solving, and talent development, her mission is to champion the world changers of tomorrow.

When she's not training for her next event, you'll find Kristy reading, enjoying craft beers, or cheering from the sidelines as the "Super Fan." Based in Chicago, you can connect with her at KristyCone.com.

THIS BOOK IS PROTECTED INTELLECTUAL PROPERTY

EASY IP ®

The author of this book values Intellectual Property. The book you just read is protected by Easy IP®, a proprietary process, which integrates blockchain technology giving Intellectual Property "Global Protection." By creating a "Time-Stamped" smart contract that can never be tampered with or changed, we establish "First Use" that tracks back to the author.

Easy IP® functions much like a Pre-Patent™ since it provides an immutable "First Use" of the Intellectual Property. This is achieved through our proprietary process of leveraging blockchain technology and smart contracts. As a result, proving "First Use" is simple through a global and verifiable smart contract. By protecting intellectual property with blockchain technology and smart contracts, we establish a "First to File" event.

LEARN MORE AT EASYIP.TODAY

www.ingramcontent.com/pod-product-compliance
Lightning Source LLC
Chambersburg PA
CBHW071432210326
41597CB00020B/3752